Key stage 3 Revision Notes

Revision Notes

Key stage 3 English

Author
KATH JORDAN

Series editor **ALAN BREWERTON**

CONTENTS

Contents

Speaking and Listening

Glossary of Literary Terms

Reading

Writing

Shakespeare

Spelling

Punctuation

Grammar

What to expect

Your final level for Speaking and Listening is decided on by your English teacher. It is based on your performance over the whole of Year 9.

The National Curriculum requires you to have experienced a wide variety of Speaking and Listening situations. You will be expected to talk about and discuss:

- plays, poetry and novels
- non-fiction texts
- personal experience
- new, unfamiliar topics.

Tasks may include:

- answering questions in class
- asking questions in class
- informal paired discussion
- informal group discussion
- formal debate
- formal paired interviews on a specified topic
- giving a talk (formal or informal)
- reading aloud
- role play or drama.

To achieve Levels 4 and 5 you need to ...

- attempt to use Standard English in formal situations
- develop ideas and sequence events through talk
- ask questions to develop ideas
- listen carefully to the opinions and ideas of others.

To move from Level 5 to Levels 6 and 7 you also need to ...

- make fluent and confident use of Standard English in formal situations
- extend your vocabulary
- listen and respond with sensitivity to the ideas of others
- engage the interest of your listener by varying pace, tone and style of presentation
- show an awareness of your audience by using appropriate language, tone and pace.

Improving your speaking and listening work

When you reach your GCSEs you will find that Speaking and Listening Assessments count for about 20% of your final grade. It is important that you practise and improve now to give yourself the best chance of increasing your levels and grades.

Talking, discussing and sharing ideas are very useful ways to improve your understanding in other areas of English. Below are some ideas for improving your performance in some of the areas listed above.

- **Asking questions** – this is an excellent way to improve your levels of understanding. Asking a question does not always mean that you don't understand what your teacher is talking about. If you do understand everything you should still ask questions. This will allow you to explore new ideas and challenge more obvious statements and concepts. It allows you to look beneath the surface for less obvious meaning. You will be given credit for asking intelligent and searching questions.

- **Answering questions** – you should always attempt to answer questions in group discussions or oral tests. Even if you get the answer wrong, you will be given credit for thinking and trying your best. If you don't feel sure of an answer you should still have a go. You may have approached the problem from another angle or thought of something that your teacher did not consider. It does happen!

Examiner's tip

If you find it difficult to speak out in front of your classmates you should begin simply, asking and answering straightforward questions first.

- **Informal discussion** – you will often be asked to discuss work in small groups (not just in English). It might be a poem, a character's strengths and weaknesses, a new approach to a problem or a social issue. The key to success is to speak **and** listen. This will allow you to share information and develop new ideas before sharing them with a larger group. You will lose marks if you remain silent and just listen. You will also lose marks if you are aggressive or you talk too much and ignore the ideas of others.

- **Formal debate** – there are rules and procedures to follow in a debate, your teacher will explain these to you. The important thing to remember is that you must use **Standard English**. Do not use slang, colloquialism or dialect words. A debate is about listening to others as well as putting your own point across. You will develop a much stronger argument if you listen and respond to the points made by the opposition. You will have prepared points before the debate begins but you won't know what the opposition has prepared. Make sure that you listen to their points and respond to them as well as putting forward your arguments.

Examiner's tip

Moving on from Level 4 – if you are not confident in Speaking and Listening then try to note down at least one point or question and make sure you use it in the debate or discussion.

- **Reading aloud** – this is a skill that can only be developed with practice. Always speak clearly and stand or sit up straight. Read to the punctuation to maintain the sense of what you are reading. Think about the content of the piece you are reading. Try to express the emotions of the characters you are reading by varying the pace and tone of your voice.

This means that you should pause or take a breath at a mark of punctuation. You should also note the difference between narrative (the story line) and conversation in a piece of fiction.

- **Role play** – take time to think about the main concerns and emotions of the character you are taking on. Try not to get distracted so that you can remain in role. Think about the style of language your character would use: formal or informal, local slang or dialect, etc.

Examiner's tip

Achieving Level 7 – if you are confident about speaking in a group, then help others by asking supportive questions to bring in weaker members of your group or by reinforcing a point made by somebody else.

Refer to this glossary as you work through the following chapters in this book.

- **Alliteration** — the repetition of a letter or letter sound at the beginning of a sequence of words. Used for emphasis and to link ideas.
  E.g. **The silver snake slithered silently by.**

- **Assonance** — the repetition of identical or similar vowel sounds in a sequence of words.
  E.g. **Silent, quiet, light, time** (long 'i' sound).

- **Caesura** — a pause in the middle of a line of poetry or a sentence in prose, for dramatic effect.
  E.g. **Angry frogs invaded the flax dam; I ducked through hedges.**

- **Empathy** — writers put themselves in the place of the person or object they are writing about; a stronger sensation than sympathy. If you empathise with someone you can understand how they feel and feel their pain, sadness, relief, etc. yourself.

- **End-stopped lines** — in poetry, a full stop or colon at the end of a line causes the reader to pause. This is sometimes used for dramatic effect, particularly when used with **enjambment**

- **Enjambment** — run on lines – when the meaning of a line 'runs on' to the next line without any mark of punctuation. Often used to show movement or excitement in a poem. See **Poetry** chapter for examples.

- **Free verse** describes a poem that has a free structure, without a regular **rhythm, rhyme, scheme or stanza** length. This form is often used in **narrative** poems to give more freedom and movement in the story-line.

- **Image** a picture painted with words. You may pick out a sensory image or an image of war, etc.

- **Metaphor** an assertion that one object is a completely different object – there is no comparison made. Similar effect to **simile** but much more powerful. E.g. **His final words were icy splinters that lodged in her heart.**

  Extended metaphor – a metaphor built up in a longer section of writing. The extended metaphor could be built using **similes** and other **images**.

- **Narrative** a story, whether told in prose or poetic form.

  First-person narrative: events are narrated by a person involved in the story.
  E.g. **I walked along the hard, stony ground.**

  Third-person narrative: events are narrated by an outside observer of the story.
  E.g. **He walked along the hard, stony ground.**

- **Narrator** the story teller. Again you could have **first-** or **third-person narrators**.

  Omniscient narrator: a third-person narrator who has access to the thoughts, feelings and eventual destiny of the characters they describe.

- ***Onomatopoeia*** the sound of a word reflects the sound that it describes. E.g. **plop, hiss, fizz, splash, etc.**

- **Oxymoron** — the joining of two words or phrases that appear to be complete opposites in meaning. E.g. **Feather of lead, bright smoke, cold fire, sick health, Still waking sleep** (Romeo and Juliet 1.i). This emphasises Romeo's dissatisfaction and confusion. He loves Rosaline, a Capulet; he should hate her.

- **Personification** — an inanimate object is given human qualities or attributes. E.g. **Well-apparell'd April on the heel/Of limping winter treads** (Romeo and Juliet 1.ii). This compares the seasons of Spring and Winter to a young lover and an old man near the end of his life.

- **Rhyme** — the ending of one word sounds the same as another E.g. **late/fate; sight/might; health/wealth.**

  End rhymes are most common. These are rhymes which occur at the end of a verse line.

  Internal rhymes occur in the middle of a line.

  Rhyme schemes are patterns of rhyme within a poem. Used for a variety of effects: to give structure; in comic verse; to link ideas.

- **Rhythm** — the pattern of beats or stresses in a line or group of lines.

- **Simile** — a comparison of two distinctly different objects using the words **like** or **as**. Used to make particular associations in the mind of the reader. E.g. **Some sat/poised like mud grenades** (a description of frogs).

- **Stanza** — a verse – a group of lines in poetry.

We read all the time! Road signs, television and films, cereal packets, newspapers, books – the list is endless! We read for different reasons: for information, for enjoyment or because we have to!

Reading is an essential part of your English course because it helps so much with other aspects of your work. The more you read, the more you can hope to improve:

- spelling
- punctuation
- the way you express yourself in writing
- understanding of texts
- analytical skills
- general knowledge.

The National Curriculum requires you to be able to read a variety of texts. They are:

- fiction
- plays
- poetry
- non-fiction
- media.

All of these areas will be covered in this section. (Plays are covered in **Shakespeare**.)

National Tests - what to expect

Paper One – you are required to:

- read an extract from a novel, short story, autobiography, biography, diary or travel writing and answer questions on it.
- read a poem or a media text and answer a question on it. Media texts could be: a leaflet, advertisement, newspaper article, etc.

Paper Two – you are required to:

- answer a question on the Shakespeare play you have studied. (You are given a mark for writing as well as reading – see **Shakespeare** section.)

About this section

In each chapter of this section you will find:

- advice about what is required to reach each level
- a text which is worked through step by step showing you what to look for
- a 'Test Yourself' section: a text with questions to work through (answers at the back of this book) and an extended question to help prepare you for the National Tests. (Answers are **not** supplied.)

Reading fiction

What to expect

Fiction can be defined as stories describing imaginary events and people. However, authors very often draw on their own life experiences and relationships when writing fiction. Perhaps this is why we can often warm to characters in novels or imagine ourselves in their situation.

Students often feel more comfortable and confident with fiction than other forms of writing. Perhaps this is because we are more familiar with this form, having been read stories from a very young age both at school and at home. Despite its familiarity, reading fiction to reach higher levels can be quite a complex task.

There is a number of elements (or ingredients) that go into making good fiction. They are:

- **plot/story-line** — a well constructed story-line will keep a reader interested as they are keen to know how a story will develop. Many novels have sub plots, minor story-lines which develop with the main plot. In a short extract it is only possible to work out what is happening at the time – you cannot comment on plot development.

- **characterisation** — writers try to know their characters very well – this helps to make them believable to the reader. We need to know what a character looks like; how they speak and behave; how they think and feel; how they get on with other characters. To maintain the flow of the plot it is not possible for a writer to directly tell us all of this information and so it is important to read beneath the surface for character development.

- **relationships** — we all have relationships – with family, friends, teachers or work colleagues. To be believable, fictional characters must develop relationships within a text. The development of a relationship can often be the central element of the plot.

- **setting** — the setting of a piece of fiction, both in time and place, is very important. Setting can often be central to creating a particular atmosphere or reflecting the mood of a character.

- use of language

interesting use of language is what makes us keep on reading. Language is not just fancy vocabulary, although a precise use of language is important. To comment on the use of language in fiction you need to recognise the use of particular devices and structures, and the extent of the detail and description.

Examiner's tip

These are the same elements that you should include in your own imaginative writing. (See **imaginative writing** chapter.)

Although all of these elements are essential to fiction writing, authors will often give more weight to one feature than to others, depending on the effects they wish to achieve.

Understanding a fiction text

To achieve Levels 4 and 5 you need to ...

- recognise what the characters are like
- have a general understanding of the whole text
- begin to read beneath the surface for meaning
- note the effect of particular words and phrases.

To move from Level 5 to Levels 6 and 7 you also need to ...

- comment on the writer's use of language
- comment on the structure of the text
- comment on the creation of setting and atmosphere
- recognise what the writer is trying to achieve and how they do this
- trace the development of plot, character and relationships
- give a personal response to the text.

When you read a piece of fiction you will notice the different elements discussed earlier in the chapter. To help organise your thoughts, ask yourself FOUR basic questions.

- WHAT is the story-line?
- WHO are the main characters?
- WHAT is their relationship?
- WHERE is it set?

Then decide which is the most important element.

The following extract is taken from 'I'm the King of the Castle', written by Susan Hill. In this section, the boy, Kingshaw, has gone for a walk in the fields and has a very frightening experience.

When you have read the extract ask yourself the FOUR basic questions and decide which is most important.

Extract from 'I'm the King of the Castle' by Susan Hill

1 When he first saw the crow, he took no notice. There had been several crows. This one glided down into the corn on its enormous, ragged black wings. He began to be aware of it when it rose up suddenly, circled overhead, and then dived, to land not very far away from him. Kingshaw could see the feathers on its head, shining black in between the butter-coloured cornstalks. Then it rose, and circled, and came down again, this time not quite landing, but flapping about his head, beating its wings and making a sound like flat leather pieces being slapped together. It was the largest crow he had ever seen. As it came down for the third time, he looked up and noticed its beak, opening in a screech. The inside of its mouth was scarlet, it had small glinting eyes.

2 Kingshaw got up and flapped his arms. For a moment, the bird retreated a little way off, and higher up in the sky. He began to walk rather quickly back, through the path in the corn, looking ahead of him. Stupid to be scared of a rotten bird. What could a bird do? But he felt his own extreme isolation, high up in the cornfield.

3 For a moment, he could only hear the soft thudding of his own footsteps, and the silky sound of the corn, brushing against him. Then, there was a rush of air, as the great crow came beating down, and wheeled about his head. The beak opened and the hoarse caw came out again and again, from inside the scarlet mouth.

4 Kingshaw began to run, not caring, now, if he trampled the corn, wanting to get away, down into the next field. He thought that the corn might be some kind of crow's food store, in which he was seen as an invader. Perhaps this was only the first of a whole battalion of crows, that would rise up and swoop at him. Get on to the grass then, he thought, get on to the grass, that'll be safe, it'll go away. He wondered if it had mistaken him for some hostile animal, lurking down in the corn.

5 His progress was very slow, through the cornfield, the thick stalks bunched together and got in his way, and he had to shove them back with his arms. But he reached the gate and climbed it, and dropped on to the grass of the field on the other side. Sweat was running down his forehead and into his eyes. He looked up. The crow kept on coming. He ran.

6 But it wasn't easy to run down this field, either, because of the tractor ruts. He began to leap wildly from side to side of them, his legs stretched as wide as they could go, and for a short time, it seemed that he did go faster. The crow dived again, and, as it rose, Kingshaw felt the tip of its black wing, beating against his face. He gave a sudden, dry sob. Then, his left foot caught in one of the ruts and he keeled over, going down straight forwards.

7 He lay with his face in the coarse grass, panting and sobbing by turns, with the sound of his own blood pumping through his ears. He felt the sun on the back of his neck, and his ankle was wrenched. But he would be able to get up. He raised his head, and wiped two fingers across his face. A streak of blood came off, from where a thistle had scratched him. He got unsteadily to his feet, taking in deep, desperate breaths of the close air. He could not see the crow.

8 But when he began to walk forwards again, it rose up from the grass a little way off, and began to circle and swoop. Kingshaw broke into a run, sobbing and wiping the damp mess of tears and sweat off his face with one hand. There was a blister on his ankle, rubbed raw by the sandal strap. The crow was still quite high, soaring easily, to keep pace with him. Now, he had scrambled over the third gate, and he was in the field next to the one that belonged to Warings. He could see the back of the house. He began to run much faster.

9 This time, he fell and lay completely winded. Through the runnels of sweat and the sticky tufts of his own hair, he could see a figure, looking down at him from one of the top windows of the house.

10 Then, there was a single screech, and the terrible beating of wings, and the crow swooped down and landed in the middle of his back.

11 Kingshaw thought that, in the end, it must have been his screaming that frightened it off, for he dared not move. He lay and closed his eyes and felt the claws of the bird, digging into his skin, through the thin shirt, and began to scream in a queer, gasping sort of way. After a moment or two, the bird rose. He had expected it to begin pecking at him with his beak, remembering terrible stories about vultures that went for living people's eyes. He could not believe in his own escape.

The text explained

- **Story-line** — the boy, Kingshaw, is chased through a cornfield by a crow. He falls and the crow lands on his back. His screams finally scare it away.

- **Characters** — Kingshaw and the crow; someone, probably Hooper, is watching from the window.

- **Relationship** — hunter (crow) and hunted (Kingshaw).

- **Setting** — isolated cornfields.

- **Most important** — the extract centres on the character of Kingshaw. It is entirely from his point of view – his thoughts, feelings and actions. Much of the tension is created by giving us access to his fevered imagination.

The writer is trying to create an atmosphere of tension and fear. To look at how this is achieved we should return to the basic elements of fiction described earlier.

- **Plot/story-line** – in this section the story is exciting and dramatic. It is a story of being chased or followed; it is told entirely from the victim's point of view so that the reader can identify closely with him. This section has a double build-up of tension. It builds up to paragraph six when the boy falls; we breathe a sigh of relief as the crow disappears. But then tension mounts when it reappears; there is a continued build-up to paragraph nine when he falls again. This time it is worse because the crow lands on him.

- **Characterisation** – the characterisation of the boy is important because it helps us understand why he is so frightened. He obviously has a powerful imagination: 'perhaps this was only the first of a whole battalion of crows' (paragraph 4). He is also presented as being sensitive to what people say and quite easily frightened: 'remembering terrible stories about vultures that went for living people's eyes.' (paragraph 11).

'Stupid to be scared of a rotten bird. What could a bird do?' The tone of this suggests that he is angry with himself for being scared. Although he seems to be quite young he is aware of his weaknesses and is critical of them.

- **Relationships** – the relationship of hunter and hunted is developed through the boy's fear. The power of the crow is increased through reference to its size: 'enormous, ragged black wings'; 'the largest crow he had ever seen'; 'the great crow'. There really isn't a relationship as such and this makes the boy seem very isolated.

- **Setting** – the setting is not the most important element in this piece of writing. The sense of menace is built up through the description of the crow rather than the surroundings. However, there is a sense that the landscape begins to turn against him: 'he felt his own extreme isolation'; 'thick stalks bunched together and got in his way'; 'it wasn't easy to run ... because of the tractor ruts'; 'a thistle scratched him'.

- **Use of language** – the way that this section is written, the use of language and structure, is what makes it powerful.

- **Repetition** – minor details become more significant because they are repeated. For example: 'the inside of its mouth was scarlet' (paragraphs 1 and 3). The structure is repetitive: he runs away and falls, then the same thing happens again.

- **Detail** – there is extensive detail about the crow, making it seem more real. There is description of what it sounds like as well as what it looks like. The detailed description of sounds made by the boy and the crow make the reader feel that there is a complete absence of background noise, highlighting his isolation: 'the sound of his own blood pumping through his ears'.

- **Structure** – the paragraphs in this extract are all quite short; this keeps the story moving at a quick pace. Some sentences are particularly short; this is a device used by writers to build up dramatic tension and suspense: 'He looked up. The crow kept on coming. He ran.'

Fiction texts

Test yourself

The following extract from 'A Kestrel For A Knave', written by Barry Hines, features Billy Casper and Mr Sugden. After losing a football match in the final minutes of a PE lesson by letting a goal in, Billy is made to have a shower before going home. Mr Sugden is angry, believing that Billy let the goal in on purpose.

Extract from 'A Kestrel for a Knave' by Barry Hines

Read the text once to familiarise yourself with the story-line. Read the questions that follow and make notes and underline parts of the text on your second reading. This will help you to answer the questions.

He thought this was funny, Billy didn't. So Sugden looked round for a more appreciative audience. But no one was listening. They faced up for a few more seconds, then Billy turned back to his peg. He undressed quickly, bending his pumps free of his heels and sliding them off without untying the laces. When he stood up the black soles of his socks stamped damp imprints on the dry floor, which developed into a haphazard set of footprints when he removed his socks and stepped around pulling his jeans down. His ankles and knees were ingrained with ancient dirt which seemed to belong to the pigmentation of his skin. His left leg sported a mud stripe, and both his knees were encrusted. The surfaces of these mobile crusts were hair-lined, and with every flexion of the knee these lines opened into frown-like furrows.

For an instant, as he hurried into the showers, with one leg angled in running, with his dirty legs and huge rib cage moulding the skin of his white body, with his hollow cheek in profile, and the sabre of shadow emanating from the eye-hole, just for a moment he resembled an old print of a child hurrying towards the final solution.

* * * * * *

While he worked on his ankles and heels Sugden stationed three boys at one end of the showers and moved to the other end, where the controls fed into the pipes on the wall. The wheel controlling the issue was set on a short stem, and divided into eight petal-shaped segments. A thermometer was fixed to the junction of the hot and cold water pipes, its dial sliced red up to 109 °F, and directly below the thermometer was a chrome lever on a round chrome base, stamped HOT. WARM. COLD. The blunt arrow was pointing to HOT. Sugden swung it back over WARM TO COLD. For a few seconds there was no visible change in the temperature, and the red slice held steady, still dominating the dial. Then it began to recede, slowly at first, then swiftly, its share of the face diminishing rapidly.

The cold water made Billy gasp. He held out his hands as though testing for rain, then ran for the end. The three guards barred the exit.

'Hey up, shift! Let me out, you rotten dogs!'

They held him easily so he swished back to the other end, yelling all the way along. Sugden pushed him in the chest as he clung his way round the corner.

'Got a sweat on, Casper?'

'Let me out, Sir. Let me come.'

'I thought you'd like a cooler after your exertions in goal.'

'I'm frozen!'

'Really?'

'Gi' o'er, Sir! It's not right!'

'And was it right when you let the last goal in?'

'I couldn't help it!'

'Rubbish, lad.'

Billy tried another rush. Sugden repelled it, so he tried the other end again. Every time he tried to escape the three boys bounced him back, stinging him with their snapping towels as he retreated. He tried manoeuvring the nozzles, but whichever way he twisted them the water still found him out. Until finally he gave up, and stood amongst them, tolerating the freezing spray in silence.

When Billy stopped yelling the other boys stopped laughing, and when time passed and no more was heard from him, their conversations began to peter out, and attention gradually focused on the showers. Until only a trio was left shouting into each other's faces, unaware that the volume of noise in the room had dropped. Suddenly they stopped, looked round embarrassed, then looked towards the showers with the rest of the boys.

The cold water had cooled the air, the steam had vanished, and the only sound that came from the showers was the beat of water behind the partition; a mesmeric beat which slowly drew the boys together on the drying area.

The boy guards began to look uneasy, and they looked across to their captain.

'Can we let him out now, Sir?'

'No!'

'He'll get pneumonia.'
'I don't care what he gets, I'll show him! If he thinks I'm running my blood to water for ninety minutes, and then having the game deliberately thrown away at the last minute, he's another think coming!'
There were signs of unrest and much muttering amongst the crowd:
'He's had enough, Sir.'
'It was only a game.'
'Let him go.'
'Shut up, you lot, and get out!'

GLOSSARY

- **The final solution** — During WW2 Hitler and the Nazis decided to kill all Jewish people. Often this was done by gassing in mass showers.

Questions

1 **WHAT** is the story-line?

the boy, Billy lets a goal in, during the last minute of the football match and his PE teacher gives him a cold shower before he can go home

2 **WHO** are the main characters?

Mr Sugden (PE teacher), Billy Casper, 3 boys he block him from getting out of the shower.

3 **WHAT** is their relationship?

Teacher and pupil.

4 **WHERE** is it set?

In the boys changing rooms at school.

5 Which is the most important element?

the extract centres on Billy and his feelings and the relationship between him and his teacher.

6 What evidence is there that Mr Sugden is taking revenge?

He won't let Billy out of the cold shower and wants him to suffer. "I don't care what he gets, I'll show him!"

7 How does the reaction of the boys change?

At first he boys were laughing and wouldn't let Billy out but then they start to feel for him and get concerned.

8 What impression are we given of Billy?

He is dirty after the match, he is a weak boy and very lonely.

READING
FICTION

LEVEL 7

READING FICTION

9 What impression are we given of Mr Sugden?

He is a bully and a poor looser. Just because Billy let a goal in he has to punish him. All he thinks about is himself and football.

10 Read the paragraph beginning: 'For an instant...' Why does the writer use this image? How is it effective?

The writer is comparing Billy to a young Jewish boy in WW2 and the PE teacher being a Nazi. As Billy runs to the shower the writer tries to make it sound like he is running to his death.

Using the work you have already done, try to write more extensively to answer these questions.

1 What kind of teacher do you think Mr Sugden is? Give reasons for your answer.

Think about:

- **what he does and how he speaks to people**
- **the way he sees his job.**

2 How does the writer make us feel increasingly sorry for Billy Casper?

Think about:

- **the way Billy is described**
- **how Mr Sugden and the other pupils treat him**
- **the way he reacts.**

Reading poetry

What to expect

Many students think they 'can't do poetry' – they worry about it, perhaps because it is less familiar than other forms of writing. We feel comfortable with fiction, advertising and newspaper reports because we see them around us all the time.

When trying to understand poetry, it is important to remember that it is simply another means of communicating. A poem is written by another human being wanting to communicate ideas, feelings, memories, hopes and dreams. It may seem less obvious than other forms of writing but this is just because poems are often more compact and less expansive than fiction, for example.

Understanding a poem

To achieve at Level 4 and 5 you need to ...

- understand what the poem is about
- begin to look for layers of meaning beneath the surface of the text
- understand ideas and feelings in the poem
- notice the effects of particular words and phrases.

To move from Level 5 to Levels 6 and 7 you also need to ...

- comment on the effective use of words and phrases and particular devices of language
- locate and comment on the use of imagery
- comment on the structure of the poem
- trace development within a poem
- give a personal response to the poem and what you think the poet has achieved.

You shouldn't expect to understand everything about a poem after a first reading; it will be packed full of emotions, ideas and images. Reading a poem involves detective work – you have to look closely under the surface for clues.

Try reading a poem through THREE times, each time looking for a different set of clues.

Examiner's tip

REMEMBER, just like a painting or a piece of music, a poem can be responded to in many different ways. So long as you can justify (back up and explain) your opinion you can't go wrong!

- **1st READING** the general meaning and story-line of the poem (if it has one)
- **2nd READING** feelings and emotions contained in the poem
- **3rd READING** interesting images contained in the poem.

Now read this poem written by Seamus Heaney. Read it through THREE times and see if you come up with the same ideas as those over the page. The notes that have been made on this poem will also be discussed over the page.

Death of a Naturalist ← meaning?

All year the flax-dam festered in the heart
Of the townland; green and heavy headed
Flax had rotted there, weighted down by huge sods.
Daily it sweltered in the punishing sun.
Bubbles gargled delicately, bluebottles
Wove a strong gauze of sound around the smell. ← sensory images
There were dragon-flies, spotted butterflies,
But best of all was the warm thick slobber
Of frogspawn that grew like clotted water ← simile
In the shade of the banks. [Here, every spring
I would fill jampotsful of the jellied
Specks to range on window-sills at home,
On shelves at school, and wait and watch until
The fattening dots burst into nimble-
Swimming tadpoles.] ← long sentence Miss Walls would tell us how
[The daddy frog was called a bullfrog
And how he croaked and how the mammy frog
Laid hundreds of little eggs and this was
Frogspawn.] ← voice You could tell the weather by frogs too
For they were yellow in the sun and brown
In rain.

As you work your way through this section remember to use the GLOSSARY on pages 7–9

Then one hot day when fields were rank
With cowdung in the grass and angry frogs
Invaded the flax-dam; I ducked through hedges
To a coarse croaking that I had not heard
Before. The air was thick with a bass chorus.
Right down the dam gross-bellied frogs were cocked
On sods; their loose necks pulsed like sails. Some hopped:
The slap and plop were obscene threats. Some sat
Poised like mud grenades, their blunt heads farting.
I sickened, turned, and ran. [The great slime kings
Were gathered there for vengeance and I knew
That if I dipped my hand the spawn would clutch it.]

Seamus Heaney

time
war images
onomatopoeia
simile
short sentence
comic book image

The poem explained

- **1st READING** — The poem is about a young boy (the poet) interested in nature, particularly frogspawn; he collects it and watches it grow. One day he is frightened by the frogs; he imagines they are going to attack him. He runs away; this ends his interest in nature.

- **2nd READING** — Stanza one: fascination with nature and wildlife

  excitement waiting for hatching; fond memories of childhood

  Stanza two: fear of big frogs; revulsion at their appearance; terror and hatred

- **3rd READING** — 'bubbles gargled delicately'
  'gauze of sound'
  'clotted water'
  'mud grenades' – images of war
  'The great slime kings'

Examiner's tip

You should have very similar answers for your first and second readings. However, as the third reading is about personal response, it doesn't matter if your ideas are different.

Making notes on a poem (underlining and highlighting, etc.) is a helpful way of organising your thoughts about it. Below you will find more detailed explanations of the notes made on '*Death of a Naturalist*'.

- **Title: Death of a Naturalist** – the title is confusing, we expect to read about a death, instead we find the story of a young boy's fascination with frogspawn. As we read on we discover that the death is not literal (real), it is symbolic (represents something else). A naturalist is a person who is interested in nature and wildlife, the young boy in this case; the death is of his interest in nature. After the encounter with the frogs he is no longer a naturalist.

  LEVEL 7

  This poem is about 'rites of passage', the move from childhood into adulthood. The poem could also symbolise the 'death' of childhood innocence. The innocent view of the goodness of nature is destroyed, never to be regained.

- **Time** – the references to time in this poem are very interesting. In the first stanza all the times are general: 'All year', 'every spring'. The first stanza describes a general interest in nature. It also shows that the collecting of frogspawn is something he does every year and that he is very familiar with the area he describes, having visited it often: 'Daily it sweltered…'.

  The reference to time in the second stanza is a signpost for the move from **general** enjoyment to a specific event at a specific point in time: 'Then one hot day…'.

- **Sensory images** – this is an image that draws on one of your five senses (touch, taste, smell, sight and hearing). There is a variety of sensory images in this poem. They are used to give the reader a sense of actually experiencing the same thing as the poet and sometimes to trigger 'sensory memories'. This sounds complicated but what it means is that if you have ever put your hand in frogspawn, the description should make you remember what it actually felt like.

  To move on a level (Level 6/7) try to think of other reasons why sensory images may have been used. For example, he is writing about childhood experiences. Children learn through their senses – every new sound, smell and taste is remembered. The 'warm thick slobber/Of frogspawn' is, perhaps, connected to a memory of a dog licking a hand or face!

Think about the language used to express these images. For example: 'bubbles gargled delicately' – this is not the language of a young child. It shows that this is a mature adult fondly remembering, perhaps romanticising, his past.

You could perhaps try to explain the contradictions of a 'gauze of sound' and 'clotted water'. Why did he use these images?

- **War images** – notice the use of words connected to war in the second stanza. The young boy feels as though the frogs have formed an army to fight back against the theft of frogspawn. He feels as if he's about to be ambushed: 'I ducked through hedges'.

- **Comic book image** – 'the great slime kings' are the product of a young child's overactive imagination just like monsters that hide under your bed! Where the first stanza contained sophisticated language and images from adulthood, this seems to come straight out of a nightmare or a comic strip, reflecting the raw terror felt at the time. He doesn't *think* the spawn might clutch his hand, he *knows*.

- **Poetic voice** – most of the poem is written in the voice of the poet remembering his youth but lines 16–19 are the voice of Miss Walls, his primary school teacher. The change of voice adds variety and it also shows that these words have stayed in his memory.

- **Similes** – if you pick out similes you must also explain why they are effective. For example: 'poised like mud grenades'. This show that the poet found them threatening and unpredictable, likely to explode (jump) at any time. It also reflects the colour and shape of the frogs.

Examiner's tip
Make sure you can spell it if you use it!

- **Onomatopoeia** – words like 'slap' and 'plop' give his writing immediacy because they make the reader feel as if they can hear the threatening sounds that the young boy heard.

- **Sentence structure** – in the second stanza sentences are quite short, particularly the one highlighted: 'I sickened, turned, and ran.' Short sentences are used to build up dramatic tension and suspense.This sentence comes as the threats have built to a peak and the young boy decides to run away.

LEVEL 7

This sentence is broken into even shorter units by the use of commas, giving a moment's pause for thought before each action. This use of short sentences is in contrast to the rambling thirty-four word sentence in the first stanza. To best understand the effect of the sentence which begins: 'Here, every spring' you should go back to it and read it out loud.

Examiner's tip

REMEMBER to read the punctuation. In other words, only take a breath when there is a punctuation mark.

You should be feeling slightly out of breath now! As you read that section of the poem you find yourself speeding up to fit all the words in before you run out of breath. This is intended to reflect the excitement and anticipation of 'watching and waiting' for the hatching of the frogspawn. It also copies the final burst into life described at the end of the sentence. The technique of enjambment keeps the poem moving forward rather than breaking up the action with unnecessary commas and full stops.

You shouldn't feel daunted by such a detailed explanation of the poem. It covers most of the elements that you could pick out of the text. You would not be expected to write at such length.

Go back to the poem and the explanations and pick out the parts that you feel most comfortable with, then try to look for those elements in other poems that you read. Build up gradually, looking for different elements each time you read.

The basic areas covered above are:

- **Title**
- **Imagery**
- **Language devices**
- **Poetic voice**
- **Structure**
- **Personal response.**

Examiner's tip

Notice there is always discussion of the effectiveness of devices and images. A key difference between Level 4 answers and Higher Level answers is the ability to locate devices and features and the ability to comment on their effectiveness.

Poetry

Test yourself

Read through this poem THREE times and make any notes you think would be helpful. Then answer the questions that follow. Questions 1, 2 and 3 should be answered after each reading of the poem.

Blackberry Picking

Late August, given heavy rain and sun
For a full week, the blackberries would ripen.
At first, just one, a glossy purple clot
Among others, red, green, hard as a knot.
You ate the first one and its flesh was sweet
Like thickened wine: summer's blood was in it
Leaving stains upon the tongue and lust for
Picking. Then red ones inked up and that hunger
Sent us out with milk-cans, pea-tins, jam-pots
Where briars scratched and wet grass bleached our boots.
Round hayfields, cornfields and potato-drills
We trekked and picked until the cans were full,
Until the tinkling bottom had been covered
With green ones, and on top big dark blobs burned
Like a plate of eyes. Our hands were peppered
With thorn pricks, our palms sticky as Bluebeard's.

We hoarded the fresh berries in the byre.
But when the bath was filled we found a fur,
A rat grey fungus, glutting on our cache.
The juice was stinking too. Once off the bush
The fruit fermented, the sweet flesh would turn sour.
I always felt like crying. It wasn't fair
That all the lovely canfuls smelt of rot.
Each year I hoped they would keep, knew they would not.

Seamus Heaney

GLOSSARY

- **Bluebeard** — A pirate who killed many of his wives by chopping off their heads.
- **Byre** — A cowshed.
- **Cache** — A hidden store of treasure, provisions or weapons.

READING
POETRY

Questions

1 1st READING: What is the poem about?

The young ~~g~~ boy goes Blackberry picking, late August with friends every year. He stores is berrys and they rot. He is upset and dosen't find it fair

2 2nd READING: What are the main feelings and emotions in the poem?

Stanza 1 - Blackberry picking. Taste sweet and made him hungry. There hands were sore because of thorn pricks. Stanza 2 - He felt like crying because the berries went off and he didn't think it fair. He hoped they would keep but he knew they wouldn't

3 3rd READING: What are the images or phrases that interested you most?

A glossy puple clot, hard as a knot, flesh was sweet, wet grass bleached our boots, burned like a plate of eyes, peppered, a rat grey fungus,

4 Make a list of words and phrases used to describe the berries in the first stanza.

A glossy purple clot, hard as a knot, it's flesh was sweet, like thickened wine, dark blobs burned like a plate of eyes,

5 Choose a phrase from the list – comment on its effectiveness.

A glossy purple clot - this is effective. It describes the berries a shiny and juicy and makes you feel like you want to eat it.

6 How are the words 'Bluebeard', 'hoarded', and 'cache' linked? Why did Heaney choose to use this image?

7 In the last three lines the tone of voice is different. Where does this voice come from and why is it effective?

8 Look at the section beginning 'then red ones inked up' and ending 'a plate of eyes'. Comment on the effectiveness of the sentence structure and the choice of vocabulary.

LEVEL 7

Examiner's tip

Try reading the section out loud to yourself, making sure you read to the punctuation

Using the work you have already done, try to write more extensively to answer this question.

1 How does the poet recreate his memories of childhood in this poem?

Think about:

- **the way actions are described**
- **the emotions he felt**
- **why the poet might have wanted to write this poem**
- **whether you think it is an effective description of childhood.**

Reading non-fiction texts

What to expect

A non-fiction text is something that is based on fact or involves a true story. However, the boundaries between fiction and non-fiction are becoming more and more blurred. There have always been historical novels to read but now we are able to watch 'docu-soaps' on television and new words like 'faction' and 'news fiction' have become commonplace media terms.

As a result of this blurring around the edges, you will find that you need to look for many of the same features as you would if you were reading a fiction text.

The kind of non-fiction texts that you might expect to find in your test are listed below. There is also a brief explanation about why they are written and what to look for in each.

- **media texts** — see next chapter.
- **autobiography** — a personal life story. The author selects and reconstructs events from their own life to share with the public. We should remember when reading an autobiography that no one has total recall of their entire life and a personal account of the subject's own life is bound to be biased. The events from a person's past are, of course, recounted with hindsight, allowing us to see the lessons that have been learned from those events.
- **biography** — a written account of a person's life, written by someone else. There are two kinds of biography: **authorised** and **unauthorised**. An **authorised** biographer has the permission of the subject to write their life story. Often the biographer will have been asked by the subject to write about them and may have spent many hours discussing the events to

be included. This will affect the way they recount particular events.

Unauthorised biographies are written without the permission of the subject. They are generally thought to be less reliable. The biographer relies on information from people who know the subject and from more widely-available sources. Some might claim that this kind of biography could be more accurate, as the writer is under no obligation to hide anything that could be embarrassing or damaging.

- **diaries** you may keep a diary or a journal. Would you like thousands of people to read it? Diaries are a record of personal thoughts, feelings, hopes and dreams. One of the most famous and widely-read diaries is that of Anne Frank. Her father allowed its publication after her death in a concentration camp. Her writings have been an inspiration to people all over the world. When we read a diary we should always remember that it is an intensely personal document, not at all like a biography that was always intended for publication.

- **letters** like diaries, private letters are personal documents not initially intended for publication. Public letters, written for newspapers or widespread circulation are, of course, very different and may aim to persuade us of something or change our opinions.

- **travel writing** although people have long been fascinated with travel, 'travel writing' is a newly popular genre. It is as much about people and personal struggle as it is about the places they have travelled to. Travel writing is often designed to entertain as well as inform. This form of writing can be compared with diaries, as accounts of journeys often begin as personal journals.

Understanding a non-fiction text

To achieve at Levels 4 and 5 you need to ...

- find information and ideas in a text
- show a basic understanding of the text
- note the use of particular words and phrases
- be aware of why a text has been written.

To move from Level 5 to Levels 6 and 7 you also need to ...

- comment on use of language and layout (if appropriate)
- show awareness of what the writer is trying to achieve and how they do it
- say how successful you think the writer has been
- give a personal response to the text.

Remember that texts written by one person about their own personal experiences are bound to be biased. Some elements may be given more emphasis whilst others are hardly mentioned. As you develop your understanding of non-fiction texts, a key skill will be the ability to recognise when you, as a reader, are being manipulated. It is important to try to keep the facts in mind, to take a balanced view and to work out exactly what the writer wants you to think and feel. As you improve your reading skills you will find it easier to do this and to see how and why a writer achieves his or her aims.

When you read a non-fiction text, begin by asking yourself FOUR basic questions.

- WHO is it aimed at?
- WHY has it been written?
- WHAT is the main idea/message in the text?
- HOW is that message put across?

The following extract is from Nelson Mandela's autobiography '*Long Walk To Freedom*'. This includes his rural African upbringing; his involvement in the struggle against apartheid; his thirty-year imprisonment and finally his election as president of South Africa. This extract is taken from the section called 'Robben Island: the dark years' and describes his prison life.

When you have read it, ask yourself the FOUR basic questions.

Extract from 'Long Walk to Freedom" by Nelson Mandela

In the midst of breakfast, the guards would yell, 'Val in! Val in!' ('Fall in! Fall in!'), and we would stand outside our cells for inspection. Each prisoner was required to have the three buttons of his khaki jacket properly buttoned. We were required to doff our hats as the warder walked by. If our buttons were undone, our hats unremoved, or our cells untidy, we were charged with a violation of the prison code and punished with either solitary confinement or the loss of meals.

After inspection we would work in the courtyard hammering stones until noon. There were no breaks; if we slowed down, the warders would yell at us to speed up. At noon, the bell would clang for lunch and another metal drum of food would be wheeled into the courtyard. For Africans, lunch consisted of boiled mealies, that is, coarse kernels of corn. The Indians and Coloured prisoners received samp, or mealie rice, which consisted of ground mealies in a soup-like mixture. The samp was sometimes served with vegetables, whereas our mealies were served straight.

For lunch we often received *phuzamandla*, which means 'drink of strength', a powder made from mealies and a bit of yeast. It is meant to be stirred into water or milk, and when it is thick it can be tasty, but the prison authorities gave us so little of the powder that it barely coloured the water. I would usually try to save my powder for several days until I had enough to make a proper drink, but if the authorities discovered that you were hoarding food, the powder was confiscated and you were punished.

After lunch we worked until 4, when the guards blew shrill whistles and we once again lined up to be counted and inspected. We were then permitted half an hour to clean up. The bathroom at the end of our corridor had two seawater showers, a saltwater tap and three large galvanized metal buckets, which were used as bathtubs. There was no hot water. We would stand or squat in these buckets, soaping ourselves with the brackish water, rinsing off the dust from the day. To wash yourself with cold water when it is cold outside is not pleasant, but we made the best of it. We would sometimes sing while washing, which made the water seem less icy. In those early days, this was one of the only times when we could converse.

Precisely at 4.30 there would be a loud knock on the wooden door at the end of our corridor, which meant that supper had been delivered. Common-law prisoners used to dish out the food to us and we would return to our cells to eat it. We again received mealie pap porridge, sometimes with the odd carrot or piece of cabbage or beetroot thrown in – but one usually had to search for it. If we did get a vegetable, we would usually have the same one for weeks on end, until the carrots or cabbages were old and mouldy and we were thoroughly sick of them. Every other day we received a small piece of meat with our porridge. The meat was usually mostly gristle.

For supper, Coloured and Indian prisoners received a quarter loaf of bread (known as *katkop*, that is, a cat's head, after the shape of the bread) and a slab of margarine. Africans, it was presumed, did not care for bread as it was a 'European' type of food.

Typically, we received even less than the scanty amounts stipulated in the regulations. This was because the kitchen was rife with smuggling. The cooks – all of whom were common-law prisoners – kept the best food for themselves or their friends. Often they would lay aside the tastiest morsels for the warders in exchange for favours or preferential treatment.

At 8pm the night warder would lock himself in the corridor with us, passing the key through a small hole in the door to another warder outside. The warder would then walk up and down the corridor, ordering us to go to sleep. No cry of 'lights out' was ever given on Robben Island because the single mesh-covered bulb in our cell burned day and night. Later, those studying for higher degrees were permitted to read until 10 or 11pm.

The text explained

- **WHO** — It is aimed at people interested in politics; apartheid and the struggle against it; general interest, Mandela being a very well-known figure around the world.

- **WHY** — To maintain the author's sense of identity in times of trouble (much of it was written whilst still in prison). To make people aware of the struggle against apartheid and how people suffered. To make sure people don't forget how things were and to ensure more progress is made.

- **WHAT** The harshness of the regime; prejudice in the prison; that it is possible to survive such hardship with dignity.

- **HOW** A factual and detailed account told without emotion; comparisons of food to highlight prejudice.

This description of daily routine is used to show that basic human rights were only just attended to in this prison. It also clearly shows that the system was run on prejudice. That is the main message of the text – now we need to look more closely at how it is put across to the reader.

- **Relationships** – the writer has used this book as a way of communicating with others. This extract shows that communication with other prisoners was rare: 'In those early days, this was one of the only times we could converse'. This extract also shows that relationships with the guards were poor: 'In the midst of breakfast ... Val in! Val in!'; 'the guards blew shrill whistles'; 'a loud knock on the wooden door'; 'ordering us to go to sleep'. All of these quotations show that there was no conversation between prisoners and guards, just the shouting of orders.

- **Food** – all of the prison meals are described in detail. Each time there is a description of the differences in rations for Black prisoners and Coloured and Indian prisoners. This is done to highlight prejudice in the system. 'The samp was sometimes served with vegetables, whereas our mealies were served straight.'

- **Sanitation** – arrangements for washing are described in great detail, again done to highlight how poor the conditions were.

- **Punishment** – in this extract punishments are not described but it is made clear that minor offences are punished severely: 'If our buttons were undone ... punished with either solitary confinement or the loss of meals.'

LEVEL 7

- **Routine** – there are many references to time in this extract and meals are described in great detail. This indicates that daily routine was important, perhaps for keeping track of time. It also shows that there was little of interest happening in normal days. Does the writer find routine a comfort?

- **Coping strategies** – there are some clues in this extract as to how the prisoners coped with the harsh regime. They are to do with communication and stimulating the brain: 'We would sometimes sing while washing, which made the water seem less icy.'

Examiner's tip

Notice that all of these comments are backed up with direct quotation or close reference to the text. In your tests you will be instructed to 'refer to words and phrases to back up your ideas'.

LEVEL 7

- **Tone** – although the writer is describing 'a dark time' in his life, the tone is very matter of fact and not at all self-pitying or exaggerated. This makes the reader more inclined to believe that the details are true and the harshness of his existence has not been dramatised for impact.

Non-fiction texts

Test yourself

In this extract the writer describes part of her journey through Zaire. Villagers were often hostile, fearing that she was involved in the slave trade. Although she made the journey alone and on foot, she did have two back-up drivers, Blake and Bill, who feature in this passage.

Read this extract carefully and read the questions that follow. As you read the extract a second time, make notes and underline details that will help you to answer the questions.

Extract from 'On foot through Africa' by Ffyona Campbell

1 I was the constant focus of their attention. The boys went ahead through one village and I passed along ten minutes later to find the people still standing together in the centre staring after them. I came behind them, a white, undefended, feeling like a beetle walking into a dawn patrol of ants. An old man broke the silence with a barrage of shrill words. The crowd broke and re-formed around me, their shrill whooping getting louder and louder until it was a throbbing wall of sound. I daren't turn.

I walked out of the village and I waved goodbye. Ten minutes later the hill behind was teeming with bands of children, whooping and hollering, their demands growing louder and louder. The tension needed relieving so I turned and smiled. They closed around me, getting excited. The ringleader grabbed at my necklace, demanding to know what it was.

2 'It is a present from my husband,' I said. 'Thank you for escorting me to him – he is waiting ahead.' And luckily both of them were.

Getting into camp was a relief not just because it meant I was safe but because I was not the only thing they were baiting any more.

3 A couple of boys would arrive first to watch the camp from a distance. Then more would come, just standing a small distance away. As the group grew, they merged into a crowd and became cocky. They were kids who'd found a new toy, and they loved to bait, to mess with it to see what it would do. They did this to me on the road – imitating me, shouting at me, and then a stone would be thrown. Blake had to defuse this in camp; I had to defuse this on the road. In camp, we could usually get them to leave in the early stages by picking out one and staring at him – this made them very self-conscious and they'd turn and leave.

4 On the road, I would turn around suddenly and growl with my hands out like claws. The children would scatter like impala changing direction. Some would take a look back at a distance and when they saw me laughing, they would laugh too and run back to hold my hand and dance along. But, after a short while, they wanted to do it again – as kids do – and the group would be gradually replaced as I walked through a long village, kids getting bored with it and falling back, to be replaced by new ones who started the baiting again.

5 The young teenage girls were the worst – they imitated my gait and would not respond to my games or return my smiles; they just sniggered. Teenage girls are the same the world over. There were times when I couldn't get the kids to laugh, possibly because I wasn't exuding the right presence. Then the stoning would be vicious. It is humiliating to be stoned, to be physically and symbolically chased out. I couldn't run; I couldn't stop them by stoning them back; I couldn't reason with them; I couldn't often get the adults to help. I was crying inside. Sometimes they hollered like Red Indians, a disorientating sound that made me feel like a hunted animal. I wondered if it was, indeed, a form of hunting. I hummed a Vangelis tune to make me feel like I wasn't actually there, just watching myself in a movie.

Questions

1 WHO is it aimed at?

People who like adventures and expeditions.

2 WHY has it been written?

To show her feelings of the terrible experience she went through.

3 WHAT is the main message/idea in the text?

It is dangerous to travel alone because anything can happen to you.

4 HOW is that message put across?

She uses lots of phrases to show how scared she is. She starts it off on the first line by saying "I was the constant focus of their attention" This must have been terrifying for her.

5 Make a list of the things that the villagers do to her.

"They closed around her", "...grabbed her necklace". "They loved to bait + mess with her". "A stone was thrown". "Snigger" "stared" "...imitating" "...shouting"

6 Make a list of the things she does to try to stop the problems.

"...waved goodbye". "...turned and smiled". "...picking out one and staring at him". "...growl, with my hands out like claws".

7 Make a list of words and phrases from the text that show how she feels.

White, undefended, terse, felt unsafe, crying inside, felt like a hunted animal,

8 Find a simile in paragraph 1. Why is it effective?

"feeling like a beetle, walking into a dawn patrol of ants" she maybe bigger than the children (a beetle is bigger than ants) but when you get a huge crowd of them attacking you it is scary.

9 Look at the sentence beginning 'I couldn't run..' (paragraph 6).

LEVEL 7

Which phrase is repeated? Why is this effective?

Can you comment on the structure of this sentence?

10 Why does she describe the children as running away like impala?

11 Read the final sentence. Why does she do this?

12 What do you think of the writer of this passage?

Using the work you have already done, try to write more extensively to answer these questions.

1 How do we know how the writer is feeling from the first paragraph?

2 After reading the whole passage, what impressions do you get about the writer's relationship with the villagers?

Reading media texts

What to expect

Media texts are all around us – we read them all the time. Media texts include your favourite soap opera, blockbuster movies and bill board adverts that we drive past every day. However, for your exams you will need to concentrate on printed texts.

Media texts are mostly intended to **persuade**. They aim to persuade us:

- to buy something
- to do something
- to change our opinion about something.

In the case of newspapers they also aim to inform us and perhaps entertain us.

In your exam you might expect to find these media texts:

- **newspaper/magazine article** — aim to inform, entertain, change opinion
- **information/advice leaflet** — aim to give information or advice on a particular topic; to change reader opinion; to help reader
- **advertisement** — aim to attract attention; to persuade reader to buy a product or service
- **holiday brochure** — aim to persuade reader to buy a holiday
- ***open letter from a charity*** — aim to involve reader in their work; to persuade reader to give money.

Understanding a media text

To achieve at Levels 4 and 5 you need to ...

- be able to locate information and ideas in the text
- be aware of the purpose of the text
- note the importance of layout features
- note the use of particular words and phrases.

To move from Level 5 to Levels 6 and 7 you also need to ...

- comment on the way layout features have been used
- comment on the way particular language devices have been used
- say how successful the writer has been in achieving their purpose
- give a personal response to the text.

Examiner's tip

To achieve at the Higher Levels you must always explain WHY and HOW a device of language or layout has been used rather than simply stating that it has been used.

A glossary of media terms

In order to write about media texts you need to make use of the correct vocabulary. The following is a list of features you may find in these texts and a short explanation of why they are used.

- **Audience** – the readership that a text is aimed at. In advertising, a lot of market research is done so that products can be aimed at very specific groups of people.
- **Bold print** – darker print makes important information stand out from the rest of the text.
- **Broadsheet** – a newspaper, considered to be more factual and serious than a **tabloid**. Aims to inform and report, not to entertain. Broadsheets are the larger of the two newspaper styles. Examples: *The Guardian* and *The Times*.

- **Bullet points** — often marked out with an asterisk or small symbol, these short sentences or phrases attract the attention of a busy reader.

- **Columns** — newspaper and magazine articles are set out in columns; leaflets sometimes use this format too. Columns break up a page and make it more interesting to look at.

- **Font styles** — different styles of printing are used to make text look different or attractive. Sometimes a particular font may be used to link it to the subject of the text.

- **Frames and borders** — sections of text may be boxed in to highlight their importance or to group together text that covers the same topic.

- **Graphs and charts** — used to demonstrate the facts in a clear visual way; they can be used to back up claims made in text and can be quite dramatic.

- **Headlines** — in newspapers they are particularly important attention grabbers. They are made deliberately dramatic so that the audience will read on. In **tabloid** newspapers, headlines are often linked to **pictures** to take up the majority of the front page.

  in leaflets, **headings** are used to attract the attention of the reader and make them read on.

  language devices such as **alliteration, rhyme** and repetition are often used.

- **Personal pronouns** — in persuasive writing, particularly advertising, the pronouns **you** and **we** are used extensively. This is to make the reader feel that they are being addressed individually and personally. This also works in charity appeals. E.g. **You** could make a difference if **you** give just £5.

- **Pictures** – in newspapers they are used to back up and dramatise or personalise a story – they are often closely linked with **headlines**.

  in leaflets they can be emotive: a picture of a lonely pensioner or a starving African child.

  in advertising, the picture can be more important than the text. They can be tempting and colourful or more stylised, perhaps black and white.

- **Quotations** – a direct comment taken from someone involved in the newspaper story. This gives the report validity and can often give a more personal feel. Reporters are required to be unbiased and give a balanced account of the story, but the people involved will often be on one side or another.

- **Short paragraphs** – long paragraphs can be off-putting for a busy reader. Most media texts are organised into short paragraphs to hold attention.

- **Slogans** – main use is in advertising. It is a 'catchphrase' linked to a product, aimed to stick in the minds of the target audience. Slogans make use of language devices such as: **alliteration**, e.g. The Totally Tropical Taste; **repetition**, e.g. Have a break. Have a Kit Kat; **puns**, e.g. Bakers born and bred, and **questions**, e.g. Have you had your Weetabix?

Note the use of personal pronouns.

- **Subheadings** are like signposts to the important information in any text. Key words and phrases are picked out to focus the reader's attention.

- **Tabloid** this kind of newspaper is considered to be less serious and, sometimes, less factual than a **broadsheet**. As well as reporting, these papers also aim to entertain. Examples: *The Sun* and *The Mirror*.

- **Text size** important information is in larger print; less appealing information – terms and conditions, for example – tend to be smaller.

- **Tone of voice** this often indicates the emotions and feelings that the writer wishes to put across to the reader. Examples of tone of voice could be persuasive, conversational, informative, tempting, dramatic or conspiratorial. You would not expect the tone to be aggressive or superior as this would put the reader off.

- **Topic sentence** the first sentence of a newspaper story, closely linked to the **headline**. It usually tells you who, what, when and where the story happened.

Later in this chapter, you will find some examples of how to comment on these features in an exam. If you can locate some of these features in a text you could hope to achieve Level 4 or 5. However, you must say how and why they are used if you wish to move to Levels 6 and 7.

When you read a media text, begin by asking yourself the same FOUR basic questions as when reading non-fiction.

- WHO is it aimed at?
- WHY has it been written?
- WHAT is the main idea/message in the text?
- HOW is that message put across?

Now study the leaflet below very carefully. It was produced by a leading supermarket chain to encourage healthy eating. When you have read it, ask yourself the FOUR basic questions.

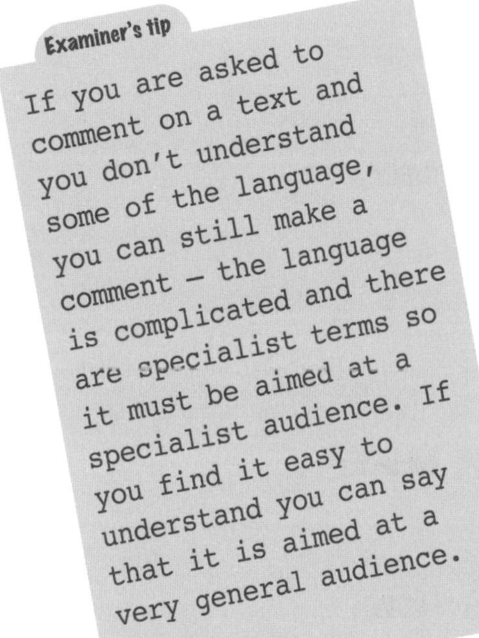

Examiner's tip

If you are asked to comment on a text and you don't understand some of the language, you can still make a comment – the language is complicated and there are specialist terms so it must be aimed at a specialist audience. If you find it easy to understand you can say that it is aimed at a very general audience.

Take 5!

Healthy Eating with Fruit and Vegetables

Healthy Eating with Fruit and Vegetables

If you have been put off changing the way you eat because healthy eating advice in the past has told you what you should not eat, here's the good news. There are many delicious foods that you can eat more of - fruit and vegetables.

Fruit and vegetables are full of vitamins, minerals and fibre which are needed to maintain good health. They are also very low in fat.

Experts agree a diet low in fat and rich in fruit and vegetables (as well as starchy foods such as potatoes, bread, pasta, rice and other cereals), is best for health. So eating more fruit and vegetables helps you gain a healthier balance of foods.

Servings

Five servings can easily fit into a normal day's eating as shown below.

Don't count potatoes in your five-a-day total because although it is a good idea to eat more of them, they are classified as starchy foods along with pasta, bread, rice and other cereals.

Breakfast - glass of unsweetened fruit juice (which counts as a serving of fruit), and/or fresh fruit chopped onto your breakfast cereal = 1-2 servings

Mid-morning - fruit instead of biscuits or confectionery = 1 serving

Lunch - salad or vegetables with your meal, or fruit instead of pudding = 1-2 servings

Evening meal - as for lunch = 1-2 servings

1 serving equals:

- 2 tablespoons vegetables
- small salad
- piece fresh fruit
- 2 tablespoons stewed or canned fruit
- glass (100ml) fruit juice

Snack happy

Many people complain that it is difficult to snack healthily, but fruit in particular is the ultimate convenience or 'fast' food because much of it can be enjoyed raw and it comes wrapped in its own neat package. It doesn't take a minute to unzip a banana, which makes an excellent snack for all ages. Ring the changes by choosing fruit in season like peaches, plums and nectarines in the summer and clementines in the winter. Try dried fruit for a change - it makes an excellent snack.

- Add sliced and grated vegetables to sandwich fillings - especially good in toasted sandwiches.
- Add grated vegetables to the meat in cottage and shepherd's pie.
- Mix mashed swede and carrot with mashed potato.
- Mix mashed or puréed fruit with yogurt or fromage frais for a quick dessert.

Five-a-Day!

Most people need to double the amount of fruit and vegetables they eat, whether it be fresh, frozen or canned (without added sugar or salt) to about 400g (1lb) in order to strike the right balance. Increasing the amount has never been easier because the choice in store has never been wider. There are fruit and vegetables to suit all tastes, occasions and styles of cooking. **The easiest way to eat enough fruit and vegetables is to adopt the Five-a-Day rule.**

Children's choice

Give children a taste for vegetables and fruit early on to establish good eating habits for life.

- Fruit and vegetable purées are a good basis for weaning foods.
- Add grated carrots or chopped celery and other vegetables to mince when making home-made burgers.
- Use brightly coloured vegetables like tomatoes and sweetcorn to make funny faces on pizza bases.
- Dried fruit like raisins make useful snacks.
- Use fresh or canned fruit in fruit jellies.

The text explained

- **WHO** The leaflet is aimed at supermarket shoppers; people who want to diet or start a healthier lifestyle; people who are concerned about what their children eat.

- **WHY** It has been written to encourage people to eat more fruit and vegetables; to promote good health habits and to persuade shoppers to buy fruit and vegetable products from that supermarket.

- **WHAT** The main idea is that buying and eating more fruit and vegetables will improve your health.

- **HOW** There is straightforward advice about what to eat. The presentation is simple and attractive.

This leaflet really has two main purposes. Although it is presented as an advice leaflet about healthy eating, it is also unmistakably an advertisement for the products available in the supermarket. To judge its success, we need to look closely at the content, language and layout of this leaflet.

- **Content** – there is a balance of facts and opinion, allowing the writer to give factual information but to be persuasive at the same time: 'fruit and vegetables are full of minerals', 'Try dried fruit for a change – it makes an excellent snack'; 'expert opinions' to make people believe that the information is medically sound; there is an easily achievable target: 'adopt the Five-a-Day rule' with information on how to meet the target.

- **Language** – is straightforward and easy to understand. This is because it is aimed at ordinary shoppers and not a specialist interest group. The language in a healthy eating leaflet for doctors would probably contain lots of medical terms. It is written in Standard English so that everyone can understand. The **tone of voice** is informal – conversational and friendly – although it is telling people to change their eating habits it doesn't come across in this way; there are suggestions rather than orders: 'Try dried fruit...' The slogan is catchy and familiar: 'Take 5!'. This is usually connected to taking a break or relaxing so it is a 'friendly' term. When you read the rest of the leaflet you realise it is connected to the target 'Five-a-Day rule'.

- **Layout** – there is a variety of layout features used in this leaflet. **Pictures:** the front cover is a full-page picture of fruit and vegetables. It looks fresh, healthy and attractive. Inside there is a number of colourful pictures which break up the text and back up the message that fruit and vegetables can be tasty and fun. **Headings:** each of the main sections has a heading to attract attention and break up the text. **Bullet points:** suggestions for serving are broken up with bullet points making it quick and easy to read. **Columns:** used to break up the text into manageable chunks, the columns are themselves broken up with pictures.

READING
MEDIA TEXTS

Reading media texts

Test yourself

This leaflet was produced by the charity HELP THE AGED to advertise a service called SENIORLINK. Read the leaflet carefully, taking note of the language and layout features that have been used, and then answer the questions that follow. Make any notes and underlinings you need to help you answer the questions.

You need never feel alone

peace of mind at the touch of a button

At Help the Aged, we care about older people. We believe that you should always feel safe and secure in your own home, particularly if you choose to live on your own. That's why we have developed SeniorLink - an immediate response service linking you to the people who care about you. And it is available to everyone.

SeniorLink gives you greater independence, security and confidence, whilst providing your family and friends with peace of mind, safe in the knowledge that we'll always be there for you.

Using your telephone line, the SeniorLink system allows you to contact us instantly.

At the touch of a button - either on your SeniorLink unit or on your personal pendant, you will immediately be connected to our round-the-clock Response Centre, from anywhere in your home or garden. Our team of highly skilled staff will quickly respond to your need.

Whether you are anxious and want reassurance, in need of emergency assistance, or you simply want a friendly chat - we are ready to take your call, anytime, day or night.

To make it easier for you to join SeniorLink, we offer a range of flexible, affordable payment options which allow you to choose a method that's right for you.

With SeniorLink, you can live in the comfort of your own home safe in the knowledge that our service offers you:

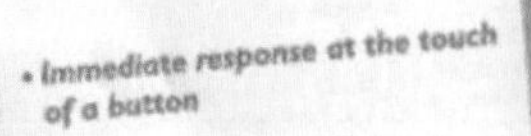

- *Immediate response at the touch of a button*
- *Contact 24 hours a day, 365 days a year*
- *Professional help from our highly trained team*
- *More than just an emergency contact - a friend to turn to anytime*
- *Greater independence, security and confidence*
- *Peace of mind for you, your family and friends.*

TEL. 01483 729678
FOR ALL ENQUIRIES

Claire Rayner sums it up:
"In a very practical and caring way SeniorLink removes a big worry. It supports our independence and the wish to live in our own home."

Test yourself

1 WHO is it aimed at?

Older people who live on their own and feel they need some security.

2 WHY has it been written?

To show older people that people care about then and want then to feel safe in their own home

3 WHAT is the main idea/message in the text?

That SeniorLink gives you ~~secu~~ security and confidence in your own home.

4 HOW is that message put across?

By Costomers that are pleased with Senior Link.

5 Make a list of the devices that have been used in the leaflet. (pictures, slogans, etc.). Use the media glossary for help.

6 List THREE facts from the leaflet.

7 List THREE opinions from the leaflet.

8 Comment on the use of pictures.

9 Comment on the tone of voice.

11 Comment on the use of personal pronouns.

Using the work you have already done, try to write more extensively to answer this question.

1 How does the leaflet try to persuade people to take part in the SeniorLink scheme?

Think about:

- **how the writer has selected information to persuade the reader**
- **the way layout and language devices have been used**
- **whether you think this leaflet will be successful.**

In school you probably think you have to do too much writing! In life we write all the time for a variety of purposes: to entertain, to persuade, to communicate complaints or praise, to inform, to make lists and notes. The list is endless!

Success in reading and writing is closely linked. Your reading in the previous section will help you to improve your writing skills. You will find that you need to refer to the **reading** section as you work through the chapters in this section.

The National Curriculum requires you to write in a variety of styles. They are closely linked to the texts you are expected to read. They are:

- **imaginative** – stories, poems and playscripts
- **non-fiction** – biographies, diaries and letters
- **media** – newspaper reports, magazine articles and advertisements
- **essays** – discussion, argument and criticism.

In this section we will concentrate on imaginative story writing and writing to inform and persuade. (This will cover most of the areas above.)

National Tests - what to expect

Paper One – you are required to:

- write about a topic which will be related to the topics from the reading sections of the paper. There will be a choice of THREE tasks. You are required to complete ONE. Tasks could include:
- imaginative writing – a story
- a piece including description of a person or a place
- a discussion essay giving your opinions about a particular subject
- a persuasive letter, leaflet or article.

Paper Two – you are required to:

- answer a question on the Shakespeare play you have studied. You are tested for reading and writing. (See **Shakespeare** section.)

About this section

In each chapter you will find:

- advice about what is required to reach each level
- a series of points giving advice on how to improve your writing
- a 'Test Yourself' section with questions to work through and an extended question to help prepare you for the National Tests. (Answers are **not** provided as all the questions require a personal response.)

Imaginative writing - stories

Imaginative writing is a form that most students feel comfortable with. This is perhaps because we are more familiar with reading fiction than other forms of writing. However, being more relaxed with this form of writing, it is easy to become lazy. Lazy writing is usually boring writing.

Examiners often comment that the imaginative sections of exam papers are the best answered. It is important to make the most of these tasks for an opportunity to score highly.

Creating a good piece of imaginative writing is similar to following a recipe. There is a number of basic ingredients that you need to include. They are:

- plot/story-line
- characterisation
- relationships
- setting
- descriptive language and dialogue.

Examiner's tip

These are the same elements that were discussed in READING FICTION TEXTS. See that chapter for explanations.

To achieve Levels 4 and 5 you need to ...

- think of an interesting story-line
- organise your writing to hold interest
- make use of interesting words and phrases
- include some conversation.

To move from Level 5 to Levels 6 and 7 you also need to ...

- create believable characters
- create atmosphere – tension and suspense, etc.
- use language for particular effects
- use structure to create effects.

How to approach imaginative writing

Before you begin to write you will need to plan and make some decisions. See **Planning** section for more details. Decide:

- what kind of story you want to write
- a basic plot outline
- third- or first-person narrative
- who your main characters are
- where the story is set.

Your writing needs clearly defined structure. This will usually take the form of three definite stages: the beginning, the middle and the ending.

The beginning

- In the opening section of a piece of imaginative writing, you need to introduce the characters and the setting, and begin to develop the main plot strands.
- It is important to create an interesting opening as you need to capture the attention of your reader.
- Do not give them too much detail. Keep them guessing so that they will want to read on. Never launch straight into 'telling a story'.
- Begin with an interesting description of a character or the setting.
- If you are writing in first-person narrative, you could begin with an intriguing statement from your main character.

LEVEL 7

- If you can handle a more complicated structure, you could begin the story with the climax of the plot and go on to look at how the events took place. You could produce a circular structure by returning to the same event at the end.

The middle

- In the central section of your writing you need to develop plot, characterisation and relationships. Development is essential if you are to hold the interest of the reader.
- Make sure you keep a balance between dialogue (conversation) and description. Too much dialogue makes your writing stilted. (Remember you are not writing a script!)
- If you made a character factfile as preparation, make sure you introduce some details from it.
- Refer back to your character plan to make sure they react to events in the way their personality suggests. If you have said they are selfish and self-obsessed, they wouldn't offer a stranger help.
- The ideas in the next section will help you to maintain the interest of the reader in the main body of your writing.

The ending

- In the final section of your writing, you must begin to tie up loose ends. You have three main options for finishing your writing:
- **Cliffhanger** – the story ends without conclusion or resolution. This keeps the reader guessing as to what will happen next. However, you need to leave some clues and have some ideas yourself for what will happen next. You should **plan** to finish in this way rather than realising you have run out of time. An unfinished ending and a cliffhanger ending are two completely different things!

LEVEL 7

- **Twist in the tale** – a completely unexpected twist in the plot right at the end. This is an exciting way to end a story but it is also more difficult to manage.
- **Resolution** – all the loose ends are tied up and the ending is complete and definite. This would often be a happy ending but it doesn't have to be.
- Try to avoid clichéd endings. You could really ruin a good story for want of an original conclusion. For example avoid: 'Then I woke up. It had all been dream!'

How to make writing interesting

- **Adjectives and adverbs** – make use of descriptive words to make your writing interesting. E.g. He sat down at the table.✗ Wearily, he sat down at the old, worn table.✓

- **Colours** – using colour in your descriptions can make them more interesting, especially if you try to be more adventurous than using yellow, red, blue, etc.
  Here is a list of colours used by Susan Hill in the extract you read earlier: **ragged black wings; butter-coloured corn stalks; its mouth was scarlet; the tip of its black wing.**

- **Imagery** – use similes, metaphors and personification in your writing.

See Glossary for explanations and examples.

- **Senses** – include images or descriptions that will appeal to the five senses. E.g. **rubbing the damp mess of tears and sweat off his face with one hand.** (*'I'm the King of the Castle'* by Susan Hill)

- **Sentence structure** – try to vary the length and construction of your sentences. This will make your writing more interesting. It will also allow you to use sentence structure for effect. If you have been writing fairly complex sentences, then a sudden change to short, simple sentences could show sudden fear.

  Here is another extract from Susan Hill's writing: **Sweat was running down his forehead and into his eyes. He looked up. The crow kept on coming. He ran.**

  She could have written: **He looked up and saw that the crow kept on coming so he ran.** All the dramatic tension is lost in this version.

Example of Levels 5, 6 and 7 imaginative writing

- I'd sit there for hours swaying backward and forwards and forwards and backward. Crying. The floor was so cold and so hard I went numb. I was numb. All the love and all the feeling I had ever had, felt like they had gone. All my hope was lost. **[Level 5]**
- Eyes as red as fire. A body as large as the cave it had come from itself. And teeth, like giant stalagtites. It was a mountain cat. And we had awoken it. Slowly, it advanced towards us. Each step growing more fierce. Each step my heart rate doubled. **[Level 6]**
- Suddenly he lost his balance and a sudden jerk forward sent him flying over the blandly-painted side rails. ... He could no longer feel his leg. As the realisation became blindingly obvious, he tried to swim to the boat. Managing to haul himself up, another sharp pain flooded to his brain. He swung round to try and break free and that's when he saw it. **[Level 7]**

Imaginative writing - stories

Test yourself

1 Write a character factfile under the following headings:

Name Davina Marick

Age 27

Occupation Teacher

Appearance Dark skin, v. thin, long black hair, large eyes

Personality friendly, caring, generous.

Leisure swimming, friends.

Ambition to be a tv presenter

Fear the dark

Family 3 sisters

Past ______

2 Imagine you are in an unfamiliar forest. Describe FIVE things that you can see, hear, smell, taste, touch/feel.

see leafless trees, darkness, shadows, stones, smoke out of a chimney from a cottage in the distance hear Owls, cracking of twigs, rustling of leaves, a stream in the distance

smell fresh air,

taste

touch/feel

3 Write down FIVE adjectives you would use to describe the forest.

eerie, dark, lifeless, silent,

4 Write down FIVE alternatives for each of the following words:

scared terrified, unsure,

excited can't wait,

ran quickly

fell tripped

angry annoyed,

5 Write TWO sentences to describe a person walking.

6 Look out of a window at home or school. Write THREE or FOUR sentences to describe what you can see. Take account of the weather

7 Complete the following similes.

The fog hung in the air like

The wind howled like a wolf

The rain fell like bombs firing down to the ground

The sound of the owls hoot echoed in my ears like a church bell

The tree branches were withered like an old tramps skin.

The best way to improve your imaginative writing is to practise. Using some of the work you have done above, try to write more extensively to answer this question.

1 Write a story about being lost or followed in a forest. You may write in first- or third-person narrative.

Writing to inform and persuade

Students tend to feel less confident with these forms of writing. Again this is because they tend to have less experience of them. If you don't know what you are trying to achieve, you will struggle to do well.

To produce a good piece of informative or persuasive writing you need to have a clear sense of purpose. You need to know what you are trying to achieve as an end result. Usually it will be one of the following:

- communicate information or ideas
- persuade people to buy something, take part in something or change their opinion about something
- express your own opinion.

In every situation you will be targeting a specific audience. You need to keep that at the front of your mind when you write. Hopefully, this will help you to keep your writing direct and focused.

To achieve Levels 4 and 5 you need to ...

- organise your ideas in a clear way
- interest and persuade your reader
- make use of a formal style and Standard English where appropriate
- support your ideas with evidence, examples and questions
- begin to develop some of your ideas fully.

To move from Level 5 to Levels 6 and 7 you also need to ...

- make use of particular language devices for effect
- use structure to create effects
- show an awareness of the audience and purpose you are writing for.

In the **non-fiction** and **media** chapters of this book, you were advised to ask yourself four basic questions after reading a text. When you write an informative or persuasive piece, you should be able to apply those same questions to your own work. If the answers are clear then you have done a good job. Those questions are:

- **WHO** is it aimed at?
- **WHY** has it been written?
- **WHAT** is the main idea/message in the text?
- **HOW** is that message put across?

How to approach informative and persuasive writing

In the National Tests you have approximately 40 minutes to complete an imaginative task or an informative/persuasive task. You would probably expect to produce between two and three sides of imaginative writing. However, all too often students produce just ½ or ¾ of a side of writing for the other tasks. Informative writing is not an easy option and it also requires a detailed response.

Formal letters

There are many reasons why you may need to write a formal letter. For example: to apply for a job; to complain to a company; to apply for a membership or book a service; to request permission.

There are a lot of conventions to follow when you are writing a formal letter.

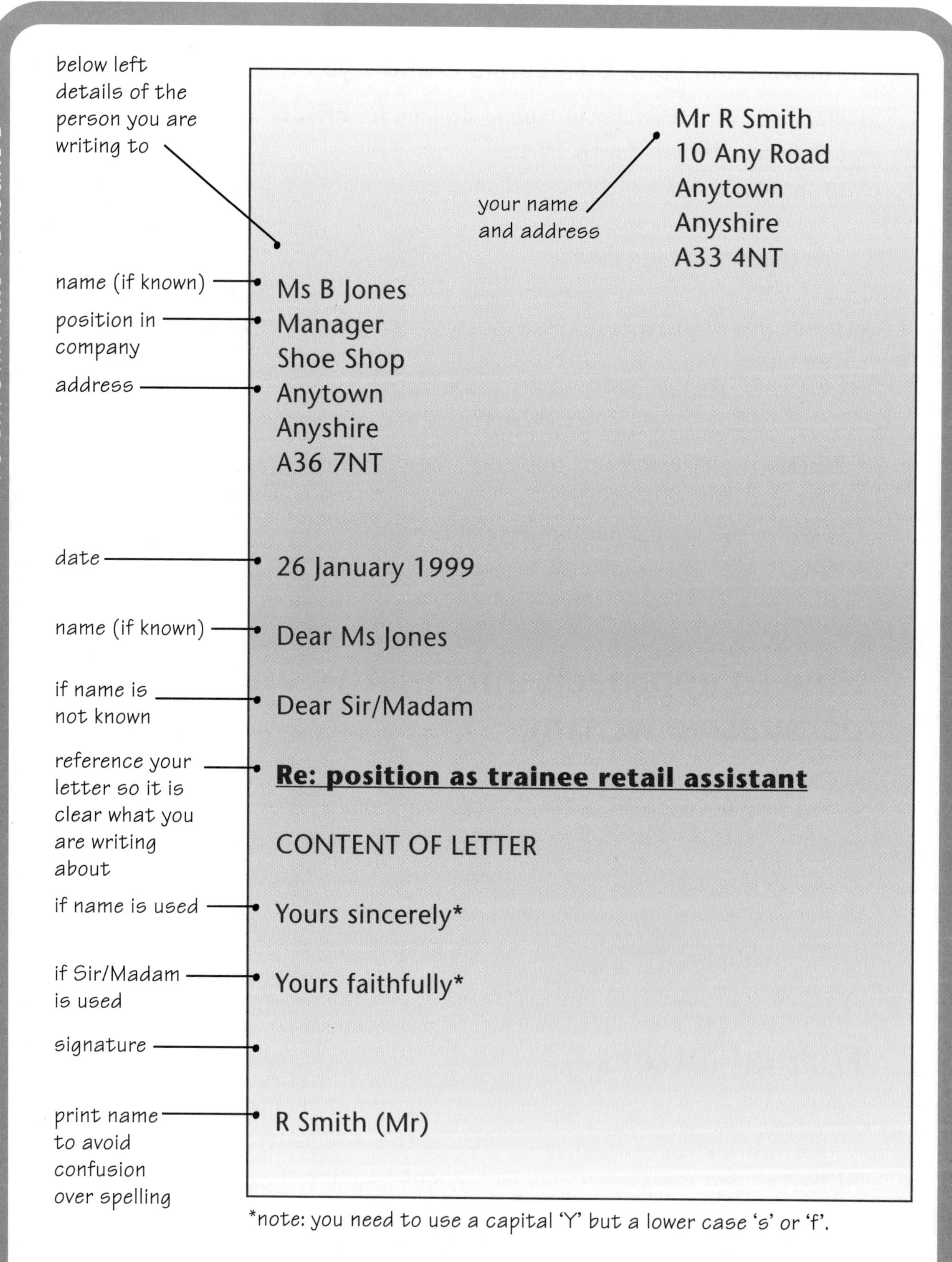

*note: you need to use a capital 'Y' but a lower case 's' or 'f'.

On many occasions when you write a formal letter, you will be writing to somebody that you have never met before. Remember the following points:

- **DO** use Standard English
- **DON'T** use slang or conversational language (colloquialisms)
- try not to be either aggressive or over-familiar in your tone
- get to your point quickly and stick to your point.

The best way to meet this final point is to plan your letter before you begin. If you were applying for a job, you would want to include the following information:

- qualifications
- experience
- personal qualities that suit me to the job
- why I want to work for your company
- interests and other experiences – about me.

Leaflets and advertisements

The best way to learn how to write in this style is to study examples of the style. Go back to the **Reading media texts** chapter of this book. The glossary and examples will tell you everything you need to know. Remember:

- you are always trying to persuade
- clever use of language is essential
- you want people to remember your main points
- you have to be concise and precise.

Essays - description argument and criticism

Description

You may approach this essay in a similar way to imaginative writing as you are aiming to produce creative and interesting descriptions of your subject. You may wish to include the following points:

- why you've chosen to write about the subject
- what you like about the subject
- how it makes you feel
- specific memories of the subject
- how you've been influenced by the subject.

Argument

There are two ways to approach such an essay:

- **A one-sided essay** – expressing your own opinions about an issue.
  Introduction – explaining the issue.
  A series of points to back up your opinion, including evidence to support your idea.
  It is essential that you have a clear argument running through your essay.
  Organise your points so that one builds on the next. Make sure you order your points to have the most impact.
  Conclusion – summing up your main points and restating your opinion.

- **A balanced essay** – considering two sides of an issue.
  Introduction – explaining the issue.
  An organised series of points in favour of the issue.
  An organised series of points against the issue.
  Conclusion – summing up the points for and against and giving your own opinion.

Criticism

- Literary Criticism is a style of writing that examines literature and explores how and why a text has been written, as well as how successful it has been. Criticism does not necessarily mean saying something is not very good. You can have a very positive critical opinion of a piece of writing.

- You will use this style of writing in the **Reading** and **Shakespeare** sections of the National Tests. Use the relevant chapters for WHAT to write and the **Planning** chapter for HOW to put together your answer.

Test yourself

1 Think of a new product name and slogan for a box of chocolates.

2 Write appealing descriptions of the following chocolates from your new range.

strawberry cream

caramel

dark chocolate with nuts

orange fondant

3 Write FIVE bullet points about the dangers of smoking, aimed at teenagers.

4 Write FIVE bullet points about safety in the home, aimed at adult home owners.

5 Write a headline and topic sentence about a lottery winner for a local newspaper.

____

____

The best way to improve your writing is to practise the styles that have been covered. Try to write extensively to answer the following questions.

1 Write a formal letter of complaint:
- you bought a box of chocolates; some were missing and the others were smashed
- you would like your money back (at least!)
- write to the Product Manager, Ms K Wright.

2 Describe a place you have enjoyed visiting. Write about:
- why you like it
- any specific memories of the place
- why you would recommend other people to visit it.

3 Write an essay about keeping animals in zoos and safari parks. Write a balanced argument – look at the points for and against.

4 Write an advice leaflet for teenagers preparing for exams. Think carefully about your presentation and layout. You should include:
- advice and suggestions for revision
- what to do in exams
- tips for relaxing.

The Shakespeare paper is the part of the test which causes most concern amongst students. Again, as with poetry, this is simply because it is less familiar and perhaps seems unconnected to modern-day concerns. However, Shakespeare's plays cover the same themes as any modern-day piece of writing. Once the barriers of language have been broken down, it is easy to see this. Shakespeare's writing covers the themes of:

- **love and relationships**
- **jealousy and hatred**
- **murder and intrigue**
- **family conflicts.**

There is nothing in this list that should be unfamiliar to modern-day readers.

National Tests - what to expect

Paper Two of the National Tests concentrates solely on your understanding of a Shakespeare play. There are three plays to choose from and your teacher will decide which one you are going to study.

In 2001 the plays are:

- Macbeth
- Henry V
- Twelfth Night

There is a choice of two scenes from each play. Again, your teacher will decide which scene to concentrate on. Although you only need to study one scene in detail, you need to have some knowledge of the rest of the play.

In Paper One, each section tests either Reading AT2 or Writing AT3. Paper Two tests both of these skills. You will be given two separate marks in this paper.

- **Understanding and Response** – this covers your understanding of the scene and the whole play you have studied. Your understanding of and response to characters, relationships and plot development is assessed.

- **Written Expression** – this assesses your ability to express meaning in your writing; the accuracy of spelling, punctuation and grammar is also tested.

In the exam there will be one question relating to each scene. Your teacher will direct you to the correct question and scene.

You can expect to find THREE different styles of question. They are:

1. **Empathy/Writing in Role** – you will be asked to imagine yourself to be a character in the scene and to write about how you feel about the events of the play you have been involved in. It is essential that you remain in role and refer to the character as 'I' or 'me'. E.g. **If I want to become king, I must kill Duncan.** **RATHER THAN: If Macbeth wants to be king ...** This will test:
   - your understanding of character emotions and reactions
   - your understanding of plot development
   - your ability to sustain writing in role.

2. **Literary Criticism** – you will be asked to write in a more detached way about:
   - how characters behave
   - how relationships are developed
   - how atmosphere is created
   - how language is used.

3 **Staging** – you will be asked to write about how a scene should be performed on stage. This will test:
- your understanding of key relationships
- your understanding of how language is used
- your ability to see the text as a piece for performance.

In the exam

You need to know your specified scene very well but you do not need to learn quotations. You will be provided with a copy of the scene with your exam paper.

If you have studied the whole play by watching a film version, make sure you do not write about events that occur only in the film.

You will never be asked simply to retell the story of the play or the scene you have studied. MAKE SURE YOU ANSWER THE QUESTION!

Always use the bullet points with the question to help plan your answer. The mark scheme is based on these bullet points.

To achieve Levels 4 and 5 you need to ...

- show an understanding of the plot
- show some understanding of the feeling and behaviour of the characters
- note the effect of particular words and phrases
- show an understanding of how your scene fits into the play.

To move from Level 5 to Levels 6 and 7 you also need to ...

- support your ideas about characters and relationships with detailed reference to the text
- write in some detail about the effects of language
- show understanding of the more complex feeling of the characters
- show an awareness of how your scene is affected by events preceding it and how it affects the action that follows.

Understanding Shakespeare's language

Rhyme and Rhythm

- **Blank verse** – unrhymed lines of **iambic pentameter**
  Shakespeare wrote his plays in blank verse because it is versatile, it is not restricted by rhyme and it is the closest to the natural rhythms of speech. This makes it easy to create different moods – anger, love, etc.
- **Iambic pentameter** – describes the number of syllables and stresses in a line, which is known as the meter. A **foot** is a pair of syllables. An **iambic foot** is an unstressed syllable followed by a stressed syllable. There are five iambic feet in **iambic pentameter**.
  E.g. **On pain / of tor / ture from / those bloo / dy hands.**
- **Rhyming couplets** – sometimes Shakespeare wrote in different styles for contrast. More formal and traditional characters making important speeches may speak in **rhyming couplets** (the lines rhyme in pairs). Because of the constraint of finding rhymes there is less movement and freedom in these speeches. This reflects the characters' formality.
- **Prose** – the 'low characters', servants for example, speak in prose rather than verse. This reflects that they have less education and their subject matter is often low or coarse.

Reflecting character or mood through language

The following examples will show you how to look closely at language for clues about character and atmosphere.

Examiner's tip

You will need to refer to the Glossary on pages 7–9.

This is an extract from Macbeth (Act 1 sc. vii lines 12–28). The witches have predicted that Macbeth will be King. He and his wife have planned to murder King Duncan. In this soliloquy, Macbeth is having second thoughts.

This means that the character is alone on stage and thinking aloud. You always hear the true feelings and fears of a character in such a speech.

He's here in double trust;
First as I am his kinsman and his subject,
Strong both against the deed; then as his host,
Who should against his murderer shut the door, 15
Not bear the knife myself. Besides this Duncan
Hath borne his faculties so meek, hath been
So clear in his great office, that his virtues
Will plead like angels, trumpet-tongued against
The deep damnation of his taking-off. 20
And pity, like a naked newborn babe
striding thc blast, or heaven's cherubin horsed
Upon the sightless couriers of the air,
Shall blow the horrid deed in every eye,
That tears shall drown the wind. I have no spur 25
To prick the sides of my intent, but only
Vaulting ambition which o'erleaps itself
and falls on th'other –

- In this speech Macbeth lists all the reasons why he shouldn't murder Duncan.

- **12–16** – the phrase **'double trust'** emphasises that Macbeth would be breaking Duncan's trust twice. He sets out the reasons logically: **1a** – he is his kinsman (relative); **1b** – he is a trusted subject; **2** – Duncan is a guest in his house so he should protect him, not plan to kill him. Macbeth presents himself with a well reasoned argument against the murder plan.

- **16–18** – these lines are more emotive. Macbeth reminds himself of all Duncan's qualities. Words like **'meek'** and **'clear'** are used to show that Duncan is virtuous and without sin.

- **18–19** – Macbeth imagines that Duncan's virtues will call out like angels, with voices like trumpets.

- **19** – **'trumpet tongued'** is an Homeric epithet, this is a compound of two words which defines a distinctive quality of a person or thing. In this case it represents a 'royal fanfare' loudly blasting the news of the murder. The fact that the angels are 'trumpet tongued' emphasises the fact that Duncan is without sin.

- **20** – Duncan's goodness is contrasted with the **'deep damnation'** of the act of murder. This is a direct comparison of the spiritual state of the two men, Duncan and his killer, Macbeth. Macbeth realises that he would be damned for eternity for such a sinful act.

Religion and the consequences of sin were very important in Shakespeare's time. The audience would regard the witches as 'agents of the devil' tempting Macbeth into sin.

- **21–25** – He uses images of innocence and purity – the new born baby and the cherubin (the highest order of angels) – as the messengers of Duncan's death. They are described as riding the winds (sightless couriers) like horses. Just as a cold wind brings tears to your eyes this news will bring tears to everybody's eyes. He imagines that the winds will be drowned with tears. This emphasises the scale of public mourning for the death of such a king.

- **25–28** – In comparison to all the reasons not to kill Duncan, his only reason to carry out the murder is his ambition. He compares his ambition to a horse that tries to jump too high and falls on the other side of the fence. Macbeth thinks that if he gives in to ambition, he will fail in the end.

- **Alliteration** is used for emphasis in this speech – **'trumpet-tongued'**, **'deep damnation'**, **'naked newborn babe'**.

- Throughout this soliloquy, Macbeth uses **euphemisms** for the murder of Duncan. E.g. **'bear the knife'**, **'his taking-off'**, **'horrid deed'**. This shows that Macbeth is reluctant to think about the brutality of the act of murder. He is trying to avoid the reality of the situation and cannot face up to the evil nature of the plan that he and his wife have made.

A less direct or harsh way of expressing an often unpleasant idea, using words or phrases that are milder or more vague.

- At the end of this soliloquy, Macbeth has convinced himself not to go ahead with the murder. This part of the soliloquy is in three sections: the reasons why the murder is wrong (lines 12–18); Macbeth's fear of discovery and eternal damnation (lines 18–25) and his want of a 'good' reason to commit the crime (lines 25–28).

How to revise

The following ideas will help you to organise your thoughts about the play you have studied. Once you have completed these tasks, the best way to revise is to answer mock questions. You will find some example questions in the **Test Yourself** section of this chapter.

- Make a time line of important events in the play. Leave space to make notes about connections between the scenes. For example:

Twelfth Night	
CONNECTIONS	EVENTS
	– Orsino is in love with Olivia
*Viola's disguise leads to unhappiness. She loves Orsino; he loves Olivia; she loves Cesario/Viola	– Viola is shipwrecked, she fears her brother, Sebastian, is dead. She plans to disguise herself as a man and serve Orsino*
	– Viola /Cesario is trusted with all Orsino's secrets and sent to woo Olivia. Viola is in love with Orsino.*
	Sebastian is rescued by Antonio
	Olivia reveals her love for Cesario*

- Make spider diagrams for the main characters to trace plot involvement, relationships and personality. For example:

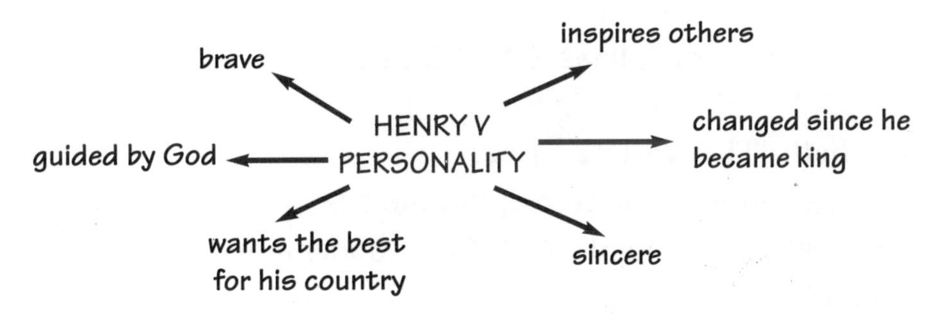

- Practise questions from the THREE question groups described on pages 68 and 69.

- Pick out the key themes in your scene and find quotations that link to this theme in other scenes. If you have your own copy of the play, mark the quotations in your text, using a different colour for each theme. If you don't have your own copy then write out the quotations and colour-code them.

Test yourself

Use the following extracts to answer Question 4.

Henry V Act 1, sc.ii, lines 222–233 and 241–245

King: Now are we well resolv'd, and by God's help
And yours, the noble sinews of our power,
France being ours, we'll bend it to our awe,
Or break it all to pieces. Or there we'll sit,
Ruling in large and ample emery
O'er France and all her almost kingly dukedoms,
Or lay these bones in an unworthy urn
Tombless, with no remembrance over them.
Either our history shall with full mouth
Speak freely of our acts, or else our grave
Like Turkish mute shall have a tongueless mouth,
Not worshipp'd with a waxen epitaph.

We are no tyrant, but a Christian king,
Unto whose grace our passion is as subject
As are our wretches fettered in our prisons.
Therefore with frank and with uncurbed plainness
Tell us the Dauphin's mind

Macbeth Act 4, sc.i, lines 94–103 and 144–154

Macbeth: That will never be:
Who can impress the forest, bid the tree
Unfix his earth-bound root? Sweet bodemonts!
Good!
Rebellious dead, rise never till the wood
Of Birnam rise, and our high-plac'd Macbeth
Shall live the lease of nature, pay his breath
To time and mortal custom. Yet my heart
Throbs to know one thing: tell me – if your art
Can tell so much – shall Banquo's issue ever
Reign in this kingdom

* * *

(aside) Time, thou anticipat'st my dread exploits;
The flighty purpose never is o'ertook
Unless the deed go with it; from this moment
The very firstlings of my heart shall be
The firstlings of my hand. And even now,
To crown my thoughts with acts, be it thought and done:
The castle of Macduff I will surprise;
Seize upon Fife; give to the edge of the sword
His wife, his babes, and all unfortunate souls
That trace him in his line. No boasting like a fool;
This deed I'll do before this purpose cool:

Shakespeare

Questions

1 Make a time line of important events in the play you are studying.

2 Make spider diagrams for each of the main characters in your scene on the following areas:
   a **personality**
   b **relationships**
   c **plot involvement.**

3 In your scene, how does the use of language help to develop atmosphere or relationships? E.g. love between two characters, humour, despair, hatred and jealousy etc.

4 a **Henry V** Act 1 sc.ii lines 222–233 and 241–245. What do we learn about King Henry's character and intentions from the language in this extract?
   b **Twelfth Night** Act 1 sc.i lines 1–15. What do we learn about Orsino's character and how he feels through his use of language?
   c **Macbeth** Act 4 sc.i lines 94–103 and 144–154. What do we learn about Macbeth's character and intentions in this extract?

5 How is the action in your scene affected by preceding scenes?

6 How does the action in your scene affect the rest of the play?

These mock exam questions are very general so that they can be applied to any scene. Try to answer these questions for your specified scene.

1 Imagine you are the central character in the scene. Write about how you feel about the events you have been involved in and what you plan to do next.

2 You are the director of the play. Write detailed instructions for how each of the main characters should be played in this scene. Think about:
- **how they should move**
- **how they should behave**
- **how they should speak**
- **what their relationships should be with other characters.**

3 Choose the most appropriate question for your scene from the list below. With all questions you should consider the following:
- **the behaviour of the characters**
- **use of language**
- **what has happened before the scene and what happens next.**

a How is the atmosphere created or changed in this scene?

b Comment on the behaviour of the main character in this scene.

c How are relationships developed in this scene?

d Why is this scene important to the play's development?

Your spelling will only be assessed directly in the final section of Paper One and in Paper Two of the National Tests. However, the more accurate your writing is, the more clearly you will be able to express your meaning.

To achieve Levels 4 and 5 you need to ...

- spell basic words and regular polysyllabic words (words with more than one syllable) correctly. In other words, you should be able to spell words that follow spelling rules and fit into patterns with other words.

To achieve at Levels 6 and 7 you also need to ...

- spell irregular polysyllabic words (words that do not fit patterns and are more commonly misspelt).

The best way to improve your spelling is to learn spelling rules, learn commonly misspelt words and PRACTISE!

Spelling Rules

The following rules will help you with your spelling. However, you need to look out for the exceptions to these rules. Unfortunately, there are quite a lot of them!

ie/ei words

- **RULE:** i before *e*, except after *c* (when the sound is **ee**).
  EXAMPLES – IE: ach**ie**ve, bel**ie**ve, f**ie**ld, rel**ie**ve, th**ie**f
  EXAMPLES – CEI: conc**ei**ve, perc**ei**ve, rec**ei**ve
  EXCEPTIONS: weird, seize, protein
  When the sound is not **ee**, you need to learn each word.
  EXAMPLES: foreign, friend, height, reign, their, weight

Prefixes

A prefix is two or three letters added to the beginning of a word to change or qualify the meaning. E.g. **dis- mis- pre- un-**

- **RULE:** When you add a prefix you do not change the spelling of the original word.
  EXAMPLES: satisfied – **dis**satisfied; spelling – **mis**spelling; necessary – **un**necessary

Suffixes

A suffix is two or three letters added to the end of a word to make a derivative of the original word. E.g. **-ed -ful -ing -ly**. Sometimes the spelling of the original word is changed by adding a suffix.

Adding -ed and -ing

- **RULE:** If the word ends in a single consonant and the syllable is stressed, you double the consonant when you add the ending. If the syllable is not stressed, you just add the ending.
  EXAMPLES: stop – stop**ped** – stop**ping**; fit – fit**ted** – fit**ting**; focus – focus**ed** – focus**ing**
- **RULE:** If the word ends in **e** you only add the **d** of -**ed**. You omit the **e** if you are adding -**ing**.
  EXAMPLES: continue – continue**d**; make – mak**ing**

Adding -ful

- **RULE:** Remember full becomes -**ful**. You do not change the original word unless it ends in **y** (see **y** ending rule).
  EXAMPLES: fit – fit**ful**; hope – hope**ful**

Adding -ly

- **RULE:** The original word does not change when you add -**ly**.
  EXAMPLES: real – real**ly**; proper – proper**ly**; careful – careful**ly**

Words ending in Y

- **RULE:** If a word ends in **y**, then you change the **y** to an **i** and add the appropriate ending. However, if there is a **vowel** before the **y**, you simply add the ending.
  EXAMPLES: fry – fr**ies** – fr**ied**; beauty – beaut**iful**; happy – happ**ily**; toy – toy**s**; play – play**ed**.

Words ending in F

- **RULE:** If a word ends in **f**, then you change the **f** to a **v** and add the appropriate ending.
  EXAMPLES: self – sel**ves**; shelf – shel**ving**; wolf – wol**ves**.
  EXCEPTIONS: There are a number of exceptions to this rule that you need to look out for. E.g. chefs, chiefs, roofs, beliefs.

Basic words

There are a number of words in the English language that sound the same but are spelt differently and have different meanings. They are known as **homophones**.

Many of these words are basic words that are commonly used in everyday writing.

The best way to ensure that you get them right is to LEARN them.

- **ARE** present form of the verb to be: **Where are you going? We are all the same age.**
- **OUR** belonging to us
- **HEAR** to perceive sound: **Can you hear me?**
- **HERE** referring to place: **Come over here.**
- **THEIR** belonging to them
- **THERE** referring to place: **It's over there.**
- **THEY'RE** they are
- **THREW** past form of throw: **He threw the ball.**
- **THROUGH** **He went through the door. I read the letter through, from beginning to end.**

Examiner's tip

The word 'THERE' has many different uses. 'THEIR' and 'THEY'RE' have only one use each. Learn the use of THEIR and THEY"RE first. THERE is used on all other occasions.

- **TO** introduces a noun or a verb: **Are you going to school? I was going to walk today.**
- **TOO** 1. also/as well: **Can we come too?**
  2. excessive: **It was too hot. That is too expensive.**
- **TWO** number 2
- **SAW** 1. past form of see: **I saw you taking it.**
  2. tool and action to cut wood: **Pass me the saw. We will have to saw the wood in half.**
- **SOAR** to fly or rise high: **The eagle soared high in the sky.**
- **SORE** painful: **My leg was sore.**
- **WEAR** of clothes, etc.: **I wear school uniform.**
- **WERE** past form of are: **We are going to school./We were going to school.**
- **WE'RE** we are
- **WHERE** referring to place: **Where is it?**
- **WHO'S** who is
- **WHOSE** belonging to

HERE, THERE and WHERE all refer to place. They are all spelt in the same way.

There are many other homophones you may need to learn. Make sure you know the following words too. **Use a dictionary to find their meanings if you don't know them.**

- bare/bear
- caught/court
- dear/deer
- fort/fought
- look/luck
- passed/past
- sea/see
- site/sight

Commonly misspelt words

- The following words are often spelt wrongly. It is a good idea to learn them as they often fail to fit into normal spelling rules.
- The parts of the words that cause confusion or difficulty have been underlined.

acceptable
accommodation
achieve
analyse
assess
believe
communicate
convenient
definite
desperate
disappear
disappoint
necessary
permanent
persuade
physical
receive
recommend
responsible
separate
stationary (not moving)
stationery (paper, etc.)
success
surprise
weird

- Use the rest of this page to list words that you have difficulty with.

When we talk, we use different tones of voice and we pause after certain words to make our meaning clear. When we write, we use punctuation to make our meaning clear.

To achieve Level 4 you need to ...

- be able to use full stops, capital letters and question marks. You should also be able to use commas within sentences.

To achieve Levels 5 and 6 you need to ...

- do all the above and use apostrophes and speech marks correctly.

To move on to Level 7...

- your use of punctuation should be accurate and should allow you to develop more complex sentence structure.

Capital letters and full stops

- show where a sentence begins and ends:
  the cat was sick in the morning we decided to take it to the vet ✘
  The cat was sick. In the morning we decided to take it to the vet. ✓
- capital letters are used for: the word 'I'
  initials, e.g. BBC, RAC
  names of people, places and products, e.g. Jane, Brazil, Weetabix.

Commas

- help us to understand the meaning within a sentence:
  John, who was very angry, shouted at the children.
  When the rope snapped, the climber fell and broke his leg.
- they are used to separate items in a list:
  You will need a pen, a pencil, a ruler and a rubber.
- NEVER USE COMMAS TO LINK SENTENCES TOGETHER.

Colons

- are advanced punctuation marks
- they point ahead to something which follows. This could be a quotation in an essay or the beginning of a list.

Semi-colons

- another advanced mark of punctuation
- used to join two sentences which are very closely linked; this may be where a full stop seems too strong and a comma too weak
- many professional writers never feel the need to use semi-colons. If you feel unsure about them then you are better not to use them. If you are aiming for Level 7, you will achieve more sophisticated sentence structure through their use
- semi-colons are also used to separate items in a list when they are phrases rather than single words
  Before you go out you should: tidy your bedroom; wash the dishes; feed the cat and hang the washing out.

Speech punctuation

Speech marks are essential in your writing to show clearly that someone has spoken. Speech marks are generally used correctly, but there is a lot more to punctuating speech than just speech marks. Here are some basic rules to follow:

- speech marks "..." or '...' are placed around the words a person actually speaks
- the first word inside the speech marks always begins with a capital letter
- the words inside speech marks always end with a mark of punctuation (full stop, comma, question mark or exclamation mark)

- if the sentence is continued after the speech marks (with he said, etc.), then you don't end the speech with a full stop, and the first word outside the speech marks must begin with a small letter
- if the sentence begins with *He said* , this must be followed by a comma before you open the speech marks
- when a new speaker begins, you must begin a new paragraph.
  'Tidy your bedroom before you go out,' said my mother.
  The man turned and whispered, 'Never ask me that again.'

Apostrophes

There are two ways to use apostrophes:

- to indicate omission
- to indicate possession.

Omission

Apostrophes are used to show that a letter, or letters, have been missed out when writing a short form. For example: **cannot** becomes **can't**.

If you remember WHY apostrophes are used then you should always get them in the right place.

People often think that the apostrophe goes between the two words that are being joined. THIS IS WRONG!

- does + not = does'nt THIS IS WRONG!
- THE APOSTROPHE TAKES THE PLACE OF THE LETTERS THAT HAVE BEEN MISSED OUT.
- does + not = doesn~~o~~t = **doesn't**
- it + is = **it's.**

Possession

Apostrophes are used to show that something belongs to someone or something. For example: **John's bag – the bag belonging to John.**

- when something belongs to a single person or thing, add apostrophe and s:
  the cat's whiskers; Sally's coat; the boy's homework.

- if the word already ends in s, then just add an apostrophe after the s:
  James' book.

- when something belongs to more than one person or thing add an apostrophe after the s:
  the cats' whiskers; the girls' bags; ladies' coats.

- if the plural form of a word does not end in s, then add an apostrophe and s:
  the children's homework; the men's hats.

- it is not just objects that belong to people: emotions, people and actions also belong.
  Susan's anger; Amanda's fear; John's father; the poet's writing.

- 'belonging to it' does not follow the above rules:
  its = belonging to it
  it's = it is.

Paragraphs

- a group of sentences linked to the same topic
- paragraphs help you to organise your work
- in handwriting, indicate paragraphs by starting a new line and indenting 1cm from the margin.

Grammar describes the way a language's sentences are put together. There are far too many rules and structures to explain here. In this section you will find some explanation about basic parts of speech.

Parts of Speech

- NOUNS — A noun is a 'naming word'. There are four groups of nouns:
- COMMON — an object you can see or touch: **pen, table, car.**
- ABSTRACT — thoughts, ideas, qualities or emotions: **peace, anger, truth.**
- COLLECTIVE — one word indicating a collection of people or objects: **group, herd, queue.**
- PROPER — an individual name; a place, a person or an object: **Birmingham, Jane, Tower of London.**

Pronouns

A pronoun takes the place of a noun that has already been mentioned: **he, she, it, me, you.** Use of pronouns helps to reduce repetition in your writing.
E.g. **John picked up the ball and threw the ball to John's friend** BECOMES... **John picked up the ball and threw it to his friend.**

Adjectives

An adjective is a 'describing word'. It tells us what a noun is like: **old** book, **sensible** child, **smelly** socks. The use of adjectives in your writing will make it more interesting.

Verbs

A verb is a 'doing word'. It makes a noun or pronoun work. There are two types of verb:

- MAIN — as a general rule you can put the word 'to' in front of a main verb: **to walk, to dance, to eat.**

- AUXILIARY — an auxiliary verb helps the main verb: You should walk to school. He could dance with Jane. I might eat the last cake.

Examiner's tip
Most adverbs end in the suffix 'ly'.

Adverbs — An adverb is a 'describing word'. It tells us how a verb is done: he walked quickly; he danced stylishly; she ate greedily.

GRAMMAR

Basic words

Test yourself

Fill in the gaps in the following sentences with THERE, THEIR or THEY'RE.

1 Your friends are over there. They're talking to the teacher.

2 The children enjoyed their party.

3 There are many helpful books in the library.

4 I like cats. They're my favourite animals.

Fill in the gaps in the following sentences with WHERE, WERE or WEAR.

5 Where have you been? I was worried.

6 What will you wear tonight?

7 The lost books were under my bed.

8 We were waiting for ages.

9 I went to a school where all pupils had to wear school uniform.

Fill in the gaps in these sentences with HERE or HEAR.

10 Come over here. I can't hear you.

11 I've been waiting here for over an hour.

Fill in the gaps in these sentences with **OUR** or **ARE**.

12 Our neighbours are from Scotland.

13 When are you going to finish your homework?

14 When will our exam results be published?

Punctuation

Test yourself

Copy out the following sentences and correct speech punctuation, capital letters etc.

1 Where are you going now asked his father

"Where are you going now?" asked his father.

2 The teacher said take this letter home to your parents

The teacher said, "Take this letter home to your parents."

3 Shut up shouted james you dont know what youre talking about

"Shut up!" shouted James, "you don't know what you're talking about."

4 I want to go home now mum whispered the bored child

5 Have you seen my sister asked simon no i havent seen her since yesterday said julie

Write out the short forms of these words using apostrophes.

1 do not........don't........

2 they will........they'll........

3 have not........haven't........

4 I am........I'm........

5 would not........wouldn't........

Copy out the following phrases adding possessive apostrophes.

1 the mans strength the man's strength

2 the workers rights (plural)

3 the suns heat

4 the girls bags (singular)

5 the girls bags (plural)

6 the clowns laughter echoed round the room (singular)

7 Lauras ambition was to be a dancer

8 yesterdays meeting was boring

9 womens shoes are more expensive than childrens

10 the company directors car was parked outside

Copy out the following sentences and add correct punctuation.

1 my sister whos a nurse helped to bandage my leg

2 the man was tall blond and wore blue jeans

3 when the bell rang the teacher dismissed the class

4 i saw james the boy who broke his leg on the bbc news last night

5 the homehelps jobs include washing the dishes ironing the clothes cooking lunch and vacuuming the stairs

Fiction - 'A Kestrel For A Knave'

pages 18–20

1 Billy is made to have a shower. Mr Sugden turns it from hot to cold because he is angry about the football game. The pupils ask him to let Billy go – he shouts at them and sends them away.

2 Billy Casper and Mr Sugden.

3 Pupil and teacher; victim and bully.

4 In secondary school – the PE changing rooms and showers.

5 The tension in the relationship between Mr Sugden and Billy is the most important element – the action centres around the relationship.

6 He puts 'guards' at the exits to prevent escape; he deliberately changes the temperature in the shower; he pushes Billy back into the shower; he accuses him of letting the last goal in on purpose; he takes no notice of the other boys asking him to stop.

7 At first they think it is funny; some of them take part in the punishment by acting as guards; when Billy goes quiet they are silenced – they gather around beginning to be concerned; they feel sorry for Billy and ask Sugden to let him out; the guards begin to feel uneasy; they are frightened.

8 He is very dirty and thin; he isn't interested in football and he can't play; he doesn't have any friends; he tries to escape; he tries to stand up to Mr Sugden.

9 He is a bully; he loves football; he likes to be in control; the other boys are frightened of him; he doesn't like Billy; he doesn't like being told what to do; he thinks he is funny.

10 The image is used to make us feel sorry for Billy, to gain the sympathy of the reader; Billy is compared to a Jewish child in a concentration camp hurrying towards his death in the shower – this is a very powerful image; because he is thin and dirty he looks like a victim – then what happens to him in the showers is like torture; it emphasises the abuse of power that is going on; if Billy is like a concentration camp victim then Mr Sugden must be compared to a Nazi killer.

'Poetry - 'Blackberry Picking'

page 29

1 Young boy (the poet) goes blackberry picking with friends; they pick lots and store them; they rot; this happens every year; he is always disappointed.

2 Stanza 1: excitement, enjoyment, sense of adventure
Stanza 2: disappointment, hopes dashed, sadness.

3 Personal response.

4 a) glossy purple clot; b) hard as a knot; c) flesh was sweet; d) like thickened wine; e) summer's blood; f) big dark blobs; g) a plate of eyes.

5 a) sounds luxurious, describes colour, shape and texture; links to image e);
b) describes texture, after pleasure of last image this makes you think of chewing on rope; rhyme with clot makes the contrast more direct;
c) flesh links to other 'life images';
d) this is an adult image; again luxurious; describes colour, texture and taste;
e) use of personification emphasises life force of summer; link to other 'life images'; also links later to Bluebeard (sticky with blood);
f/g) in contrast to d) this is a childhood image again linked to Bluebeard, sense of adventure, slightly distasteful connection enjoyed by a young child.

6 Pirates – Heaney sees himself and his friends as a band of pirate adventurers, childhood games running through the fields, the berries are as precious as treasure to him.

7 Most of the poem is about the adult looking back on childhood; this is the child's complaining, disappointed voice; adds variety; compared to sophisticated images of stanza 1, 'lovely canfuls' sounds like a child; the best way to convey the bitter disappointment he felt.

8 Long sentences and use of enjambment keep the poem moving forward; mirrors the children running through the fields, the urgency of filling up all the containers with berries; words like milk-cans, pea-tins, jam-pots are tricky to say one after the other, you have to skip over them lightly, again this reflects the movement of the children.

Non-fiction – 'On Foot Through Africa'

pages 38–39

1 People who are interested in travel and adventure; people who have organised their own expeditions.

2 To keep a personal record of her journey; to share her experiences with an interested audience; to make money!

3 The struggle to fit into a foreign culture; the dangers of travelling alone.

4 Through the sharing of personal and painful experience; this is written more emotively than the Mandela extract.

5 Close in around her; shout and question her; grab at her possessions; watch her; imitate her; throw stones; hold her hand; laugh at her.

6 Smile at them; pick one out and stare at them; growl and make claws; make them laugh.

7 A white; undefended; feeling like a beetle…; barrage of shrill words; broke and reformed around me; wall of sound; I daren't turn; demands growing louder; they closed around me; loved to bait; teenage girls were the worst; stoning would be vicious; humiliating; chased out; I couldn't…; I was crying inside; hunted animal; disorientating; I wasn't actually there.

8 'Like a beetle walking into a dawn patrol of ants'. This gives the feeling of ambush and surprise; it emphasises the feeling of being surrounded and swarmed over; it evokes the surroundings of the country she is writing about.

9 'I couldn't' is repeated; effective because it builds up feelings of helplessness and captivity; describes a series of basic danger-avoiding techniques she cannot do – frustration and fear; makes us aware of the barriers she faced. Sentence structure: seems like an endless list of things she cannot do; the use of semi-colons instead of full stops creates the feeling of problems piling up one after another.

10 Impala are native to Africa, evokes a sense of place; they are hunted by lions – she is imitating a lion; the children scattered in all directions – a herd of impala would do this if chased.

11 A defence mechanism; if she faced the reality that the terrible things were happening to her, she would have to give up.

12 Personal response.

'Media - Help the Aged Seniorlink'

page 50

1 Old people who live alone and people who are concerned about their elderly parents.

2 To persuade those people to find out more about and hopefully buy a SeniorLink package.

3 SeniorLink maintains independence for old people and peace of mind for their children or carers.

4 Information about the product, quotes from satisfied customers.

5 Pictures, direct quotations, slogan, bullet points, different font styles and sizes, balance of fact and opinion.

6 A service from Help the Aged; operates 24 hours a day, 365 days a year; works through SeniorLink telephone and call button; there are different payment options; the telephone number.

7 'You need never feel alone; peace of mind at the touch of a button; SeniorLink gives you greater independence…; we'll always be there for you; to make it easier for you…; more than just an emergency … a friend.

8 On the front cover there is a woman looking out of her window, she looks isolated and worried. There is also a call centre operator; she looks friendly and helpful. The two pictures are used together to show that there is a solution to the problem of loneliness. Inside the leaflet there are pictures of men and women wearing the SeniorLink pendants. They look happy and relaxed and you can see that the call button is small and doesn't get in the way. There is also a picture of the SeniorLink telephone to show that there isn't any complicated equipment.

9 The tone of voice is reassuring and friendly without being patronising; it offers straightforward information about what the SeniorLink package includes; it isn't a high pressure sales pitch as the next move is to get more information not to place an order.

10 The use of personal pronouns is important and makes the leaflet personalised, a direct invitation to the reader to find out more; **You** need never feel…; **We** believe that **you** should always feel safe; linking **you** to the people who care about **you**; **We'll** always be there for **you**. This would particularly appeal to older people who feel lonely or live away from their family.

11 The use of personal pronouns is important and makes the leaflet personalised, a direct invitation to the reader to find out more; 'SeniorLink offers **you**'; 'links **you** to the people who care about **you**'; '**We're** there when **you** need **us**'; this would perhaps be particularly effective for a lonely person.

Basic Words

pages 87–88

1 there, they're	2 their	3 there	4 they're	5 where
6 wear	7 were	8 were	9 where, wear	10 here, hear
11 here	12 our, are	13 are	14 our	

Punctuation

pages 88–89

1 "Where are you going now?" asked his father.
2 The teacher said, "Take this letter home to your parents."
3 "Shut up!" shouted James. "You don't know what you're talking about."
4 "I want to go home now mum," whispered the bored child.
5 "Have you seen my sister?" asked Simon.
"No, I haven't seen her since yesterday," said Julie.

1 don't	2 they'll	3 haven't	4 I'm	5 wouldn't

1 man's	2 workers'	3 sun's	4 girl's	5 girls'
6 clown's	7 Laura's	8 yesterday's		9 women's, children's
10 director's				

1 My sister, who's a nurse, helped to bandage my leg.
2 The man was tall, blond and wore blue jeans.
3 When the bell rang, the teacher dismissed the class.
4 I saw James, the boy who broke his leg, on the BBC news last night.
5 The homehelp's jobs include: washing the dishes; ironing the clothes; cooking lunch and vacuuming the stairs.

Index

The Author and Publisher are grateful to the following for permission to reproduce copyright materials: pages 14-15 *I'm the King of the Castle* Susan Hill, reproduced by permission of Penguin Books Ltd, © Susan Hill 1970; pages 18-20 *A Kestrel for A Knave* (pp 105, 106 to 108) Barry Hines, Michael Joseph, 1968, © Barry Hines, 1968, reproduced by permission of Penguin Books Ltd; pages 24-25 'Death of a Naturalist' Seamus Heaney from *New Selected Poems 1966-87* reproduced by permission of Faber and Faber Ltd; page 29 'Blackberry Picking' by Seamus Heaney from *New Selected Poems 1966-87* reproduced by permission of Faber and Faber Ltd; pages 35-36 *Long Walk to Freedom* Nelson Mandela, reproduced by permission of Little, Brown and Company (UK); pages 38-9 *On Foot Through Africa* Ffyona Campbell, reproduced by permission of Orion Publishing Group Ltd; page 47 *Take 5! Healthy Eating With Fruit and Vegetables* reproduced by permission of J Sainsbury's plc; page 50 *SeniorLink* © Help the Aged, 1998, reproduced by permission of Help the Aged.

Letts Educational
Aldine Place
London W12 8AW
Tel: 020 8740 2266
Fax: 020 8743 8451
email: mail@lettsed.co.uk
website: www.letts-education.com

First published 1998
Reprinted 1998, 1999
New edition 1999
This edition 2000

Reprinted 2000, 2001

Editorial and design by Hart McLeod, Cambridge

British Library Cataloguing in Publication Data
A CIP record for this book is available from the British Library.

ISBN 1 84085 4898

Printed in Italy

Letts Educational Limited is a division of Granada Learning Limited, part of the Granada Media Group.